July
Sean U.

With warmest regards
from the author.

Maggie enjoy this
tale of a great American.

Best wishes,
Patrick V. Garland

# A Forgotten Soldier

The Life and Times of

Major General Harry Hill Bandholtz

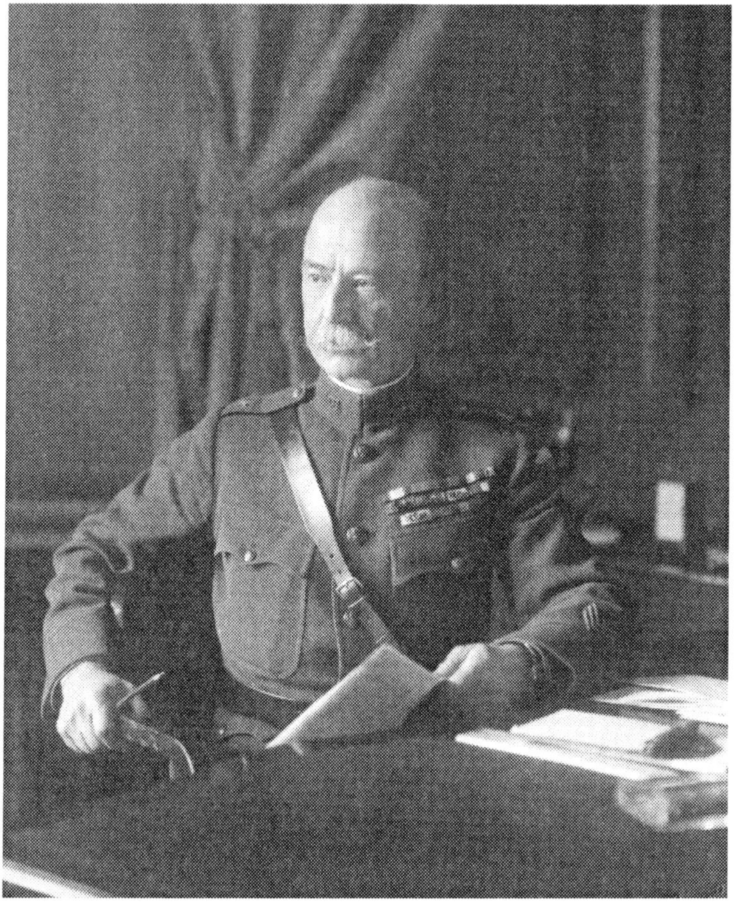

by

**Patrick V. Garland**

INFINITY
PUBLISHING.COM

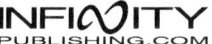

Copyright © 2009 by Patrick V. Garland

*All rights reserved. No part of this book shall be reproduced or transmitted in any form or by any means, electronic, mechanical, magnetic, photographic including photocopying, recording or by any information storage and retrieval system, without prior written permission of the publisher. No patent liability is assumed with respect to the use of the information contained herein. Although every precaution has been taken in the preparation of this book, the publisher and author assume no responsibility for errors or omissions. Neither is any liability assumed for damages resulting from the use of the information contained herein.*

ISBN 0-7414-5189

Published by:

1094 New DeHaven Street, Suite 100
West Conshohocken, PA 19428-2713
Info@buybooksontheweb.com
www.buybooksontheweb.com
Toll-free (877) BUY BOOK
Local Phone (610) 941-9999
Fax (610) 941-9959

Printed in the United States of America
Published March 2009

In memory of my brother, Chris!
He is my personal hero, a soldier's soldier!

PSG Christopher J. Garland, USA (ret)
1931 - 1971

Silver Star, Republic of Viet Nam

Bronze Star Medal, with V for Valor (2 awards), Korea and Viet Nam

Purple Heart (4 awards) Korea and Viet Nam

Combat Infantryman's Badge (2 awards), Korea and Viet Nam

"I simply carried out the instructions of my Government, and as I understood them, as an officer and gentleman of the United States Army"

Inscribed on the base of the statue of

General Harry Hill Bandholtz, Budapest, Hungary.

Contents

Acknowledgements ................................................... i

Introduction ........................................................ iii

The Early Years ..................................................... 1

Preparing For A Military Career ............................ 6

Early Military Assignments ................................... 12

Off To War ........................................................... 19

Trouble In Augusta, Georgia ................................. 39

The Philippines ..................................................... 44

Constabulary ........................................................ 54

Chief Of Constabulary .......................................... 65

Diplomacy ........................................................... 71

Mining Investments ............................................... 75

The Moros ............................................................ 78

Pacification .......................................................... 85

Back To Army Service .......................................... 90

Organizing The Military Police ............................. 99

Division Of Criminal Investigation ...................... 110

Hungary .............................................................. 117

Pressure The Occupiers ....................................... 134

The Romanian Perspective ............................... 144

The Serbs ............................................................ 148

Winding Down ................................................... 153

Return To The U.S.A. ........................................ 158

America's Unknown Soldier .............................. 165

The Knickerbocker Snowstorm .......................... 172

Military Retirement ............................................ 177

The Final Years .................................................. 182

The Statue .......................................................... 186

Postscript ........................................................... 192

Appendix One .................................................... 193

Appendix Two ................................................... 199

Appendix Three ................................................. 201

Appendix Four ................................................... 202

Appendix Five .................................................... 205

Appendix Six ..................................................... 207

Biography .......................................................... 221

# ACKNOWLEDGMENTS

This must be the hardest portion of a book for an author to write. There are so many people who contributed in some way to the project, whether or not they realize their contributions.

The story really began with my acceptance into the Criminal Investigation Division (CID), of the United States Army and the truly professional people I was privileged to work with over those next 15 years. The more I learned of my new trade, the more I wanted to know why, when and where it all started. CID and Military Police Histories mention General Bandholtz, but very briefly.

For this project, I must acknowledge the assistance given by Grafton Cook, of Michigan, a researcher who possesses a vast store of material about General Bandholtz in his memory. Thanks also to Karen Jania, Bentley Historical Library, University of Michigan, for access and permission to use from the Bandholtz Papers; Elaine McConnell, US Military Academy Library, for copying material from books in their collection and for access to academy archives; the US Army Military Police Corps Museum and Archives, Fort Leonard Wood, MO, for photographs from their Bandholtz Collection; the Hungarian Military Archives, for copies of documents in their files, Mr. Vilmos Gal, Mr. Zoltan Balaho, Ms. Katalin Bognar, and all the staff of the Hungarian National Museum, Budapest, for access to the Bandholtz Hungarian Diaries, period photographs and his artifacts; Paul E. Camp, University of South Florida-Tampa Library, for access to their collection of materials on the Spanish American War; my friend Allen E. "Gene" Barnett, for his use of the personal letters of Corporal

Norris Ball; and the Staff at the US Army Military History Institute, for copying documents from their collection. No matter where I turned, the people were courteous and generous with their time.

I would like to thank Dr. Harper Cole, and Dr. Eleanor Carter, both dear friends who proofread much of the material and offered suggestions, also to retired CID Agent Clarence Romig, who did proofreading and encouragement; Ms. Maria Cristina Serban, of Bucharest, Romania, who escorted me around her city, translated Romanian material, and pointed me in the direction to gain some Romanian perspective; Mr. Sandor Torak, History Teacher, Budapest, who transported me to the sites I needed to visit, and translated Hungarian materials; and to my lovely wife, Betty, who has stuck with me for four decades thus far. She has been beside me with this project since the beginning, and never falters in her support. Her proofreading and suggestions have been very much appreciated. Finally, I am grateful to the subject of my work, for leaving an extensive paper trail.

Patrick Garland

Sun City Center, FL

# INTRODUCTION

After World War II, Europe was divided into zones of occupation by the victors and soon became a battleground of the "Cold War." Hungary was one of those unfortunate nations swallowed up by the Soviet Regime, and a Communist government installed. Many items of nationalism, or indicating Western influence, were destroyed or removed. With the easing of tensions between East and West, segments of the "Iron Curtain" began to crumble; the start was along the Hungarian-Austrian Border, in 1989. In that same year, Hungary resurrected and re-dedicated monuments, including the statue of a US Military Officer, which had been taken down by the Communists 41 years earlier. One must wonder what such a man did to be so revered by the Hungarians, and yet remains unknown in the United States.

October 5, 1919, Brigadier General Harry Hill Bandholtz was enjoying a quiet evening meal in Budapest, Hungary. He was the American Representative to the Inter-Allied Military Mission, which was comprised of General Officers from the US, Britain, Italy and France. Their mission was to disengage the belligerent forces of Hungary and Romania, the latter having occupied much of, if not all of Hungary's land. On that particular day, he was presiding over the group.

After dinner, he was notified that Romanian Army soldiers were at the Hungarian National Museum with a number of trucks. With two of his staff, General Bandholtz rushed to the Museum, where he confronted the soldiers. The Romanians insisted they had been ordered by their high command to basically loot the museum. He ordered them away and posted an order on the museum door, which stated: "To whom it may concern – As the Inter-Allied Mission in charge of all the objects in the Hungarian National Museum at Budapest, the key has been taken charge of by the

President of the Day, General Bandholtz, the American Representative." Similar notes were posted on each of the museum's access doors.

Knowing the European fascination with rubber stamped official documents, General Bandholtz obtained an American mail censor's stamp, and affixed those stampings on the orders, to make them more "official." At the time of his confrontation with the Romanians, General Bandholtz was armed with his riding crop, although it is known that he generally carried a holstered Smith and Wesson Safety Model Revolver, in a back pocket. This action by General Bandholtz earned him a great deal of respect in the eyes of the Hungarian people.

What sort of man would expose himself to danger, in such a way, to protect the property of a foreign nation that had been an enemy of the United States just months prior? In studying his life, I find this was not an isolated instance. I found him to consistently be a stalwart, even-minded, and often-humorous individual. His riding crop is enshrined in the Hungarian National Museum, Budapest.

What he thought of the Romanian occupation of Hungary, he expressed in his own words as: "Judging from the Roumanian (sic) occupation of Hungary, our little Latin Allies have the refined loot appetite of a Mississippi River catfish, the chivalrous instincts of a young cuckoo, and the same hankering for truth that a seasick passenger has for pork and beans."

I must add a note here, that while General Bandholtz was usually very critical of the Romanians, I found that those I have met during the researching of this book have been most friendly, helpful, and fully cooperative. Additionally, I have included excerpts from books on Romania offering the Romanian viewpoint. Throughout the book I have used various titles for General Bandholtz. To simplify the story I have used Harry in place of his various grades.

# Chapter One

# THE EARLY YEARS

As we go through life we see and hear about many people who accomplish great things during their lifetimes. Sometimes it is through history books, paintings, or television documentaries, and other times we pass a statue in a park. What did these people do to earn such honors? That is a question, which often caused me to reflect on such matters.

In this case, it was the reading of a novel,[1] which started me on a search for more knowledge. The book, an action thriller, mentioned a statue located in a park situated across the street from the US Embassy, on Szabadság tér (Freedom Square), in Budapest, Hungary. It was just a brief segment in which the book's characters wondered what this man had done, since he was in the uniform of a United States Military Officer, with the name Bandholtz. This also sparked my interest. After all, Hungary was behind the Iron Curtain for most of my life. I had heard the name Bandholtz before, but knew very little about the man.

As I began to research his life I realized that here was a man who accomplished so much, in his short life's span. Through these pages, I hope to be able to do justice to a man of bravery, compassion, wit and patriotism, such as is evident in but a few. Many American military leaders are proclaimed as "heroes," and revered as such, because of some isolated or short-term incidents of bravery. Not so with General Bandholtz. In everything he did, he excelled; from leading troops in combat, to negotiating with his enemies, to organizing vast organizations with little or no resources. Today he is virtually forgotten.

---

[1] *The Hostage, pg 389, by W. E. B. Griffin, G. P. Putnam, 2005*

Harry Hill Bandholtz's statue was erected by a grateful Hungarian nation because of his contributions during the aftermath of WWI, but his life's story is filled with a variety of deeds, in a wide range of locales. Unfortunately his life was short, a mere 60 years. His life ended in the same community where he first saw light, although his life's journey saw him travel the world. He met with people at the highest levels of governments and he consorted with royalty! On the other hand, he was respected by his subordinates and often by his adversaries.

In the year 1864, the United States was engaged in a horrific civil war. Throughout the land, battles had been raging, and the soul had been torn out of the nation. Brother was fighting against brother, and the cost in lives was staggering. The Confederate Army suffered a crushing blow, in Nashville, Tennessee, and "Sherman's March to the Sea," neared Savannah, Georgia. No part of the country had been spared from the hardships. Into this set of circumstances, a young man who was destined to become another military leader was born in Michigan.

On a chilly December 14, 1861, in Constantine, Saint Joseph's County, Michigan, Christian Johan Bandholtz married Elizabeth Hill. This union was blessed with two children, a daughter Christine, and later a son, Harry Hill, born December 18, 1864. Who could have foreseen that this pink wrinkled little fellow would rise to a stature realized by so few? His father, an emigrant from Schleswig-Holstein, the border area between Denmark and Germany, was a harness maker, while his New York born mother was a milliner.[2] Christian's father, Gottlieb, was a tradesman, in carpentry and masonry, while Elizabeth's family were old American stock, with links back to Commodore Oliver Hazard Perry, US Naval Hero of the War of 1812. The Bandholtz's also ran a boarding house.

---

[2] *US-Michigan Census, 1870*

St. Joseph County is bisected by the St. Joseph River, and borders Indiana, in Michigan's southwest corner. French explorers, missionaries and fur traders traveled the St. Joseph River Valley during the seventeenth and eighteenth centuries.

A French settlement at Fort St. Joseph (present-day Niles), as well as the activities of area fur traders, kept white men interacting with Indians throughout the St. Joseph River Valley into the nineteenth century. But it was only after the opening of the Erie Canal in 1825 that St. Joseph received its first permanent white settlers.[3]

The earliest settlers were Southerners who emigrated through Ohio, arriving in 1827, enticed by rumors of vast fertile prairies. These rumors were exaggerated, as the prairies were small, numbering on average only a couple of hundred acres. They did produce grain though and St. Joseph's first water-powered gristmill was erected in 1830. Twenty-five miles away, Constantine was platted in 1831. This and other towns grew as the result of waterpower and agriculture. Great grist and sawmills, and manufacturers of farm implements arose, shortly thereafter, followed by furniture makers and foundries. These companies shipped their products via the St. Joseph River and Lake Michigan, into Eastern markets. In 1853 the first cemetery was designed and laid out. The first school was taught in the basement of a store. It was into this community where an emigrant harness maker and his wife settled and prospered.

The Bandholtz household was a very short distance from the river, and Harry's childhood included many hours swimming, fishing or boating. Young boys seem to be attracted to water at a very early age. He was small in stature, but had a strong resolve. His cohorts would not bully him. When Harry reached age 10, his family moved to Detroit, where he was educated in the Public School System.

---

[3] *St Joseph's County,* by Jane Simon Ammeson, Arcadia Publishing, 2005

This was short term, as they soon returned to Constantine. Here, again, he was involved in everything considered normal for teen-age boys. In addition, he helped his Dad around the shop, grooming customer's horses while their tack was being repaired or made.

During these formative years, one must wonder why young Harry began thinking of military service. The impetus may have been that a former product of the Constantine Public School System, Frank Dwight Baldwin,[4] twenty-two years senior to Harry, belongs to a very select group of individuals who was awarded the Medal of Honor (MOH). This Michigan native, born in Manchester, but raised in Constantine, was awarded the nations highest award for his heroic actions, on July 12, 1864, at the Battle for Atlanta, during the Civil War. While this man's charge through enemy lines, where he captured two confederate officers, and a Georgia Regiment's guidon would certainly impress a youngster, Baldwin went on to win a second Medal of Honor. The latter incident occurred on November 8, 1874, when Baldwin attacked, with two companies of his 5$^{th}$ Infantry, a vastly superior number of Indians, at McClellan's Creek, Texas to rescue two white girls who had been captured by the Indians.[5]

Upon graduation from Constantine High School, during 1881, Harry began business as a collector and later as a billing clerk. He moved to Chicago and accepted a position as bookkeeper for a large mercantile company. Big city life was a huge change to a young man from a rural area. The city was still rebuilding after the Great Chicago Fire of 1871, and was quickly becoming a very populous and important American city.

It was not long after his arrival in Chicago when Harry enlisted as a private soldier in the Illinois National Guard.

---

[4] *Major General Frank Dwight Baldwin, (26 June 1842 – 22 April 1923) a native of Constantine, Michigan, born in Manchester, Michigan,*
[5] *MedalofHonor.com:Frank Dwight Baldwin*

During his service there, he was promoted to "lance sergeant." This title is normally awarded to soldiers of inferior rank performing the duties of a sergeant. His leadership qualities were recognized early!

With this introduction to military service, Harry felt a need to take this career more seriously. He returned home to take a competitive examination for the US Military Academy, which was being held in his district. Harry took the test and wound up ahead of all other entries.[6] His appointment to West Point came through the office of Michigan's long time political power broker, Julius Caesar Burrows,[7] US House of Representatives. Mr.( later US Senator) Burrows would support Harry Bandholtz during his entire military career.

It was also in Chicago where Harry first met May Cleveland, who would later become his wife.

---

[6] *NY Evening Telegram, March 6, 1919, "Men Made by the War," Bandholtz Papers*
[7] *Julius Caesar Burrows (January 9, 1837 – November 16, 1915) was a U.S. Representative and a U.S. Senator from the state of Michigan.*

# Chapter Two

## PREPARING FOR A MILITARY CAREER

Cadet H. H. Bandholtz, Class of 1890,
by permission Military Police Museum

In preparation for his upcoming travel to West Point, N.Y., Harry enrolled in the Michigan Military Academy, a respected, all-boys military prep school in Oakland County, Michigan. He attended during the winter term of 1885-86. The school was founded in 1877 by Captain J. Sumner Rogers,[8] and closed in 1908 due to bankruptcy. During its peak years, it was known as the "West Point of the West." With a tuition of $500 per year, the academy attracted sons of wealthy upper class businessmen. There were three levels of training at the school: Infantry, Artillery, and Cavalry. The cadets wore gray and white uniforms, modeled after those that were worn at West Point.

---

[8] *Captain J. Sumner Rogers (b. 1844), who was a professor of Military Science and Tactics at Detroit High School, bought the land to establish the school.*

From there he traveled to New York. Where he begin training at the US Military Academy, West Point. In those days, the train ride across country would have taken days, with many changes of scenery. The terminus would have been in Manhattan, a very busy place at the time. Connecting trains were available to West Point, and exactly how Harry traveled is unknown. However, getting off the train and taking a riverboat was a popular option.

At the south end of Manhattan Island, riverboats were loaded for the trip up the Hudson River to West Point. This is also where inbound emigrants were landing, by the tens of thousands, from virtually every country in Europe. They were milling around, searching for relatives or friends. Others were trying to find where they would have a place to stay. Fishing fleets were off-loading their catches. Fishmongers transported their purchases over cobblestone streets, in their steel wheeled handcarts, to their markets for sale. Other ships were discharging large consignments of goods of every description. The clanging of bells, blowing of steam whistles, shouting, the screeching of winches, as longshoremen emptied the holds of cargo, made conversation difficult at best.

As the riverboat started up the normally calm Hudson River, the boisterous sounds of the city faded away, and turned to the serenity of quiet river travel. Roughly half way to West Point, the boat passed the infamous Sing-Sing Prison, situated on a bluff on the eastern shore of the river. Built in 1825, using marble quarried on-site, prisoners from another facility constructed this prison, whose original plan was to include 800 cells. At the time of Harry's trip, Sing-Sing held approximately one thousand hardened criminals. At the end of the journey, the boat disembarked its passengers in the small village of Highland Falls, New York. This was a short walk, or carriage ride, to the grounds of the West Point Reservation.

The United States Military Academy is located in Orange County, New York, about 50 miles north of New York City. The school buildings sit on the high ground on the western bank of the river. The post itself was first occupied in 1778, as a fort, and therefore is the oldest continuously occupied military post in the United States. General George Washington himself selected this site for the construction of a fort because of its commanding view of the Hudson River. Controlling the river would prevent British Warships from traveling between New York City and Canada. To aid in that venture a large metal chain was anchored at West Point stretching across the river to the eastern shore. It was Tadeusz Kosciusko [9] who designed the fortifications of the post in 1778.

Benjamin Franklin, who wanted his service in the Continental Army, initially recruited Kosciusko in France. Commissioned a Colonel of Engineers, Kosciusko designed fortifications including those at Philadelphia, and many forts along the Canadian Border, and elsewhere. He was considered one of the best military engineers of the time. Although awarded American citizenship, Kosciusko returned to Europe, where he fought in continental armies. He died in Switzerland in 1817.

Following the American Revolution, President Washington quickly realized the need for a national military academy, but his Secretary of State, Thomas Jefferson, stated the Constitution had no provisions allowing for the creation of such an institution. However, when Jefferson became the third president, he signed legislation establishing the United States Military Academy on March 16, 1802. The school was opened on July 4th of that same year.

The beauty of the grounds must have impressed Harry. Overlooking a double curve in the scenic Hudson River Valley, in the midst of surrounding green hills, the buildings,

---

[9] *Andrzej Tadeusz Bonawentura Kościuszko( 1746 – 1817) born in Lithuania, Chief Engineer of the Continental Army*

constructed of grey stone, inspired him to draw several sketches of land, buildings, and the cadet life. Harry entered the grounds a young twenty two year old, filled with determination to succeed. Living in a rural area, and use of his muscles, had him well able to handle the rigors he was to face.

Sketch of Academy Buildings by Cadet H. H. Bandholtz Bandholtz papers, UMICH

However, this fascination may have been tempered by the rude reception and harassment by "upper classmen" which falls upon all who attend the Academy, and by the examinations all candidates are required to pass. Many prospective cadets failed these first examinations and were returned home, filled with disappointment.

On his first "plebe" day, Harry was called upon to march the class, a group of youngsters from all over the country, most of whom had no marching experience whatsoever. Time spent in the Illinois Guard and at the Michigan Military Academy had prepared Harry, so he did rise to the task assigned. He was also accustomed to the feeling of inferiority one goes through, when being constantly berated by senior cadets. So many youngsters succumb to this sort of treatment, and as a result the situation only worsens.

Academically, Harry was an average student, completing his four-year term towards the middle of his class, finishing $29^{th}$ in a class of 54. Earlier, his class standing had gone from $17^{th}$, in his second year, to $32^{nd}$ in his third year. His favorite subjects seem to have been drawing (as can seen by his illustrations in this book), and languages. In his second year, he went through with no demerits, an accomplishment of significance, but he slipped some during the following year.

Cadet Corporal Bandholtz (left) by permission,
US Army Military Police Museum

First Place, in class standing went to Cadet Edgar Jadwin, (1865-1931) who was retired as Lieutenant General and served as Chief of Engineers. Second place went to Charles Keller, (1868-1949) also an engineer officer, who had the distinction of being the oldest Army Officer on active duty during World War II. He too retired as a General Officer. Their class curriculum included such subjects as: Mathematics, English, French, Philosophy, Chemistry, Chemical Physics, Mineralogy, Tactics, Civil and Military

Engineering, History, Spanish, Law, Ordnance, Gunnery and Discipline.

Within the Corps of Cadets, Cadet Bandholtz went through the ranks reaching the grade of 3$^{rd}$ Ranking Lieutenant, in his battalion formation. The officers are selected from those students being the most studious, soldier-like in the performance of their duties, and most exemplary in their overall general deportment. The Class of 1890 was graduated on June 12$^{th}$, Harry was appointed Second Lieutenant of Infantry.

That year also saw the end of Indian Hostilities, with the Battle of Wounded Knee, in December. It was unlikely then, that Harry was destined to be an Indian Fighter. The country was at relative peace.

England was fighting the Dutch, over lands in South Africa, and the Japanese had recently defeated China, but these conflicts were very far away. Of course, there always seemed to be bitter feelings and battles between occupiers and the native population. The seemingly endless risings against British rule in Ireland and India continued, and in Cuba and the Philippines, revolutionaries against Spanish Rule, were struggling for independence. Pleas had been received from the Cuban insurgents for assistance, but the American people were fed up with war, having gone through six years of a terribly costly Civil War, and the years of struggle with the Indians. The peacetime Army had been reduced to about twenty five thousand troops. The country had grown to a population of over sixty two million. Immigrants flooding the ports hoping for a new life, amounted to almost a half million during 1890 alone.

Harry though, was assigned to a quiet post in Northern New York, near the border with Canada.

# Chapter Three

# EARLY MILITARY ASSIGNMENTS

Lt H. H. Bandholtz (L), by permission
Military Police Museum

Before heading for his first post, the new lieutenant went on leave, marrying May Cleveland, on July 15, 1890, in Chicago, Illinois. Officiating at the ceremony was the Reverend M. H. Harris, Pastor of the Church of the Redeemer,.[10] May was the daughter of S. E. Cleveland, resident of Chicago.

The first year of his military career found Harry and May at Fort Ontario, New York, with the 6th US Infantry. This post was first built by the British, during the French-Indian War, in 1755, and was called "The Fort of the Six Nations," It is outside of Oswego, NY, overlooking Lake Ontario. Destroyed by French forces, and again during the Revolution, the fort was rebuilt three times before being

---

[10] *Marriage License #155090, Cook County, State of Illinois, 14 July 1890*

officially turned over to the United States in 1796, following British withdrawal from the lands east of the Mississippi as a result of the Treaty of Greenville. It was destroyed again during the War of 1812, by the British, and remained in ruins until re-garrisoned by the US in 1839.[11]

At the time of his service at Fort Ontario, Officer' Quarters consisted of two houses, each with room for two officers. Harry and May had their only child, a son, Cleveland, born in Oswego on June 13, 1891. Shortly thereafter, Harry was transferred from Company K, to Company C, 6th Infantry, at Fort Thomas, KY, where he was, in addition to his normal duties, in charge of physical training and gymnastics.

Fort Thomas came into being during 1887, to replace a military post, across the Ohio River, in Cincinnati. The land, consisting of 11 acres, was selected by General Phillip Sheridan,[12] and named in honor of General George Henry Thomas.[13] Thomas was a heroic commander of Union Forces during the Civil War, where he was given the nickname, "Rock of Chickamauga," but affectionately "Pop Thomas" by his troops. The US 6th Infantry moved here until it was called to action for the Spanish American War of 1898.[14]

During the period, May 13 to August 17, 1893, Harry was on detached service to Company I, 12th US Infantry, a company of former Apache prisoners. These men were being trained for service by Captain William H. Wotherspoon, at Mount Vernon Barracks, Alabama, located about 25 miles north of Mobile. The post was established by the United States Army in 1828 as an ordnance manufacturing base. Mount Vernon Arsenal served as one of the US Army's main ammunition plants from its inception until the Civil War. Captured by the

---

[11] *Friends of Fort Niagara Website*
[12] *Philip Henry Sheridan (March 6, 1831 – August 5, 1888) U.S. Army officer and a Union general in the American Civil War*
[13] *George Henry Thomas (July 31, 1816 – March 28, 1870) was a career U.S. Army officer and a Union general during the American Civil War,*
[14] *http://www.ftthomas.org/History.html*

Alabama Militia early in 1861, the Arsenal was turned over to the Confederate Army, when Alabama seceeded from the Union. It remained in southern hands until the war ended.[15]

The Chiricahuas, one of the most feared Indian tribes, arrived at Mount Vernon in 1887, and by 1888 virtually the entire band, including the infamous Geronimo (one who yawns), were at the south Alabama post. Born in the late 1820s, Geronimo had blood or marriage ties to at least three Apache tribes including the Chiricahuas. He came of age during a period of incessant war between the Apaches and the Mexicans. Geronimo raided villages and attacked Mexican troops, but he gained greater notoriety for his ability to lead his people away from danger. Indeed, many Chiricahua Apaches believed that Geronimo had supernatural powers, that helped them conduct guerrilla warfare against numerically superior foes. Geronimo was not the most prominent Chiricahua chief among his own people, but he came to represent Apaches to white America because his name appeared first in newspaper headlines and then in tourist circles.

When the Chiricahuas arrived at Mount Vernon Barracks, they set up camp in the forests outside the twelve-foot brick walls. The Indians helped Lieutenant Charles G. Treat survey and map the barracks. By October 1891 the company joined the battalion for parades, eight and ten-mile marches, training in advance-guard techniques, fording streams, building bridges, and skirmishing. The Indians proved to be able soldiers and were led by Chato[16] and former holdouts from Geronimo's[17] band.

While Geronimo did not volunteer his services to the Army, he was able to sign his name on Indian artifacts, mostly made as souvenirs, which were sold by traders. It appears,

---

[15] http://en.wikipedia.org/wiki/Mount_Vernon_Arsenal
[16] Chato, former Army Scout, and hero for Indian Fighter General George Crook
[17] Goyathlay (1829-1909), Chiricahua Apache War and spiritual leader

this was a lucrative endeavor for Geronimo, and many such objects, bearing his name turn up today! Harry had a number of dolls reportedly made by the great Indian Chieftain.

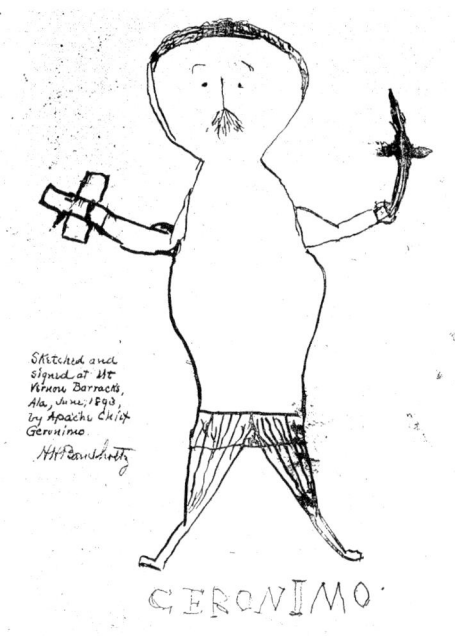

Sketch of Lt Bandholtz by Geronimo
Bandholtz papers, UMICH

Harry got to know Geronimo during this point in his career, having had several conversations with the Apache leader. It appears they had frequent meetings, as both were inquisitive men sharing similar interests. It was during one of these encounters that Geronimo drew a caricature of his soldier friend.

During the fall of 1893, Harry returned to Fort Thomas. Shortly thereafter he was on detached service to Fort Niagara, NY, as a competitor in target shooting matches, held from August 18 to September 21, and again the next year at the Fort Thomas Rifle Range, KY, his home station. Target shooting has always been required during military service, and the best shooters were encouraged to participate in competitive matches. Scoring first place during such matches, gave the winning team bragging rights, but the lessons learned during competition would also benefit the overall marksmanship program of the Army. Even today, the Army holds competition at all levels, and its teams participate in Inter-Service, National, and International Competitions. Target shooting remains a part of the Olympic Games. Shooting was so strongly supported that the United States Congress founded the Civilian Marksmanship Program, with the goal to train civilian shooters, to better prepare them for possible military service. This was extremely important for a country with a small standing Army, which relied on a call for volunteers, or a military draft, in times of emergency.

When the rifle competitions were completed, Harry returned to his normal duties, in 1895. While at Fort Thomas, Harry co-authored a book, with Lieutenant C. G. Morton,[18] Regimental Quartermaster, entitled "Manual of Military Signaling, for the use of Regular Army, National Guard, Military Schools and Colleges." This 57 page manual covered such subjects as signaling with flags, batons or wands, signal lamps, etc., construction of lines for telegraph or telephone use, the flying telegraph, submarine cables, ciphers and the use of balloons.

A short time later, he applied for duty as Professor of Military Science and Tactics, Michigan Agricultural College, East Lansing, Michigan. Receiving glowing endorsements from previous and current commanders, this request was approved.

A Military Science Department had been established in 1884, in accordance with the requirements of an act of Congress, whereby colleges receiving public lands, were required to teach military tactics. The program was under the control of an officer of the regular army, detailed by the war

---

[18] *Major General Charles Gould Morton, (1861-1933), served in the Philippines in the Spanish-American War and World War I.*

department for this duty. Such an assignment was a good sign of recognition and often resulted in advancement through the ranks.

Lieutenant H. H. Bandholtz,1897 By permission, Military Police Museum

Harry Bandholtz began his tenure with the school in 1896. At that time the Corps of Cadets were equipped with Cadet Pattern Springfield Rifles and two field pieces of artillery. An allowance of ammunition was supplied for instruction and annual target practice. The college provided the students with band instruments, swords, flags and colors; whatever was needed for training.[19]

Harry was a strict taskmaster and discipinarian. He instilled in his cadets a sense of pride, according to the West Point Code of "Duty, Honor and Country." The year 1897 still finds Lieutenant Bandholtz as Professor of Military Science and Tactics, at Michigan Agricultural College. But things

---

[19]*Catalogue, Officers and Students, Michigan Agricultural College, for the year 1896-7, published by the college*

were taking shape far from Michigan, that would alter his life.

He would soon be called back to his regiment, to make preparations for a more active service. Upon his departure from the college, all of his 200 students would give Harry and May a send off, with the band playing and all wishing him "Godspeed." May and Cleveland would return to Chicago, while Harry continued on to Tampa, Florida.

## Chapter Four

## OFF TO WAR

Drawing by Cadet H. H. Bandholtz, U.S.M.A
1886-1890

On February 15, 1898 the US Battleship Maine was blown up in Havana's harbor and war clouds were developing over Cuba. War with Spain was imminent. The explosion, causing the destruction of a US Battleship, while berthed in a Cuban port, may have been contributory, but may also have been an excuse.

There were people of power, within and without the government of the United States who were anxious to get into colonization. They wanted more expansion, and new sources of raw materials. The industrial revolution, after the Civil War, had made the United States a very powerful nation, economically. Having completed the western movement to the Pacific, the country sat secure behind its oceans, as European nations had been taking over smaller states stripping them of their natural resources. The continent of Africa was being systematically carved into colonies of the French, English, Dutch, Belgians and Germans. The Spanish had colonies across the Pacific and the Caribbean. Many of these colonies had been in constant conflict with their oppressive rulers for many years. The insurgents, notably in Cuba and the Philippines, were seeking American assistance in throwing off the shackles of Spanish rule. Cuban revolutionaries had visited Washington, to plead their case, and General Emilio Aguinaldo,[20] leader of the Filipino insurgents, was meeting secretly with American emissaries in Singapore and Hong Kong. He had hoped to sail to Manila with Dewey's Invasion Fleet, but was unable to travel to Hong Kong before the fleet departed.

While the United States did have a strong Navy, the Army had been badly depleted. There were nowhere near enough troops to take on the power of Spain. Calls for Volunteer Regiments went out, and many were responding to the call. "Remember the Maine," became a rallying cry, even though there was no real evidence that the Spanish had anything to do with her sinking. The volunteers would need arms and equipment, and those were in short supply. Obsolete weapons were distributed, while orders were issued for uniforms , and all other material required for war.

During April of 1898, before war with Spain was declared, President McKinley[21] sent for Colonel Arthur Wagner,[22] head of the Army's Bureau of Military Intelligence. The President, worried over the prospect of war, realized he needed information regarding the Spanish forces in Cuba and the condition of the insurgent Cuban forces. Telling him

---

[20] *Emilio Aguinaldo y Famy. (1869-1964), Filipino General and President*
[21] *William McKinley, (1897-1901), 25$^{th}$ President of the United States*
[22] *Colonel Arthur Wagner (1853-1905), Head, Bureau of Military Intelligence*

about a letter he had for General Garcia,[23] head of the Cuban irregulars fighting the Spanish in Cuba, McKinley asked whom could he send to deliver the message? Arthur immediately responded with "There is a young officer here in Washington; a lieutenant named Rowan, who will carry it for you!"[24] McKinley's response was "Send him!"

Wagner gave his orders to Arthur Rowan, a West Point Graduate of 1881, who was able to depart almost immediately. He was transported by railroad to New York where he boarded a ship to Jamaica. At Kingston, he was met by Cubans, and escorted to an unknown location where he was secreted aboard a small fishing boat, sailing the one hundred miles to the Cuban coast. With his guides, he landed spending several days trekking through the jungles of the island, he was taken to General Garcia's Headquarters. Only then did he remove an oilskin pouch, strapped to his chest, opened it and handed the McKinley letter to the general.

He planned to stay in Cuba, to obtain intelligence on Spanish positions and fortifications, but Garcia suggested that instead he should return to the United States with some of his trusted aides, who could provide all the needed intelligence. Lieutenant Rowan, with his new allies, crossed to the northern shore of Cuba where they were provided with a small skiff, gunny sacks for sails, and meager rations for the crossing to America. Off the coast of New Providence, in the Bahamas they were stopped and quarantined, but contact with the American Consul had them quickly released. They landed in Key West, May 13th, transported by train to Washington, where they made their reports. For his deeds,

---

[23] *General Calixto García e Iñiguez ( 1839 – 1898) , Cuban revolutionary*
[24] *Lieutenant Andrew Summers Rowan, (1857-1943), 19th Infantry Regiment*

Lieutenant Rowan was later awarded the Distinguished Service Cross.[25]

The intelligence, gathered from this mission, confirmed that the Spaniards greatly outnumbered the American troops available for the invasion. However, rather than being in large formations, they were scattered throughout the island of Cuba, manning fortified "blockhouses," which seemed to be situated on every highpoint. The largest would hold less than a thousand troops.

Rowan's mission became well publicized through a magazine article, entitled "A Letter to Garcia," written by a Elbert Hubbard, in February 1899.[26] Published as a "filler" in a monthly magazine, it soon caught the attention of employers who wanted it to inspire their workers. It was reprinted in millions of copies, in several different languages.

While Lieutenant Rowan was on his mission, war had been declared against Spain. The US Pacific Squadron, under the command of Commodore George Dewey, sailed from Hong Kong, with orders to find and destroy the Spanish Pacific Fleet. At dawn, May 1, 1898, Dewey located the Spaniards in Manila Bay, the Philippines engaged them, destroying the fleet in a matter of hours. No American ship was destroyed or severely damaged, and not a single sailor was lost in the battle. Spain lost a number of capital ships, and hundreds of her seamen.

Back in Cuban waters, the Cruiser Marblehead and Gunboat Nashville, dispatched small boats, manned by volunteers, to get within 60 yards of Cienfuegos. In order to assist with the eventual Cuban landing, they were to dredge up and cut three underwater cables, which allowed communication between Cuba and Jamaica, and then through relay to Spain. The

---

[25] *How I Carried the Message to Garcia, by Colonel Andrew S. Rowan,* http://www.arlingtoncemetery.net/asrowan.htm
[26] *Elbert Green Hubbard (June 19, 1856 – May 7, 1915) American writer, publisher*

operation, conducted within range of riflemen on shore, took several hours, and cost the lives of several sailors, but was successfully completed on May 11, 1898, a full month before the invasion force was able to depart from Tampa.[27]

Days later, Harry received the following orders, "*Special Orders No.114, Headquarters of the Army, Adjutant General's Office, Washington May 16, 1898. Para 9 By direction of the President, $1^{st}$ Lieutenant Harry H. Bandholtz, $7^{th}$ Infantry, is relieved by the Secretary of War, from duty at the Michigan Agricultural College, Lansing, Michigan, and will proceed to join his company. The travel enjoined is necessary for the public service. By Command of Major General Miles.*"

Attached was a "Depot Quartermaster's Office voucher, dated May 21, 1898, for transportation from Chicago, Illinois to Tampa, Florida with sleeping car accommodations."[28]

Prior to the receipt of these orders, however, Lieutenant Bandholtz had written, offering his services to the Michigan National Guard, to the Governor of Michigan, Hazen S. Pingree. Volunteer Regiments were being raised for the war. Although accepted, Lieutenant Bandholtz put this on hold so that he could go to Cuba with his permanent regiment.

It should be pointed out here that State Militias were not Federal Troops, and could not be used as such in foreign wars. Therefore, those states wishing to contribute troops, to serve in foreign countries in time of war, formed Volunteer Units, staffed by their own officers, and attached to larger Federal Armies. It was into this type organization, where Harry sought to serve.

Probably the best well known Volunteer Regiment formed for Spanish American War Service was the $1^{st}$ United States Volunteer Cavalry Regiment, known as the "Rough Riders." Assistant Secretary of the Navy, Theodore Roosevelt, was

---

[27] *The Cable Cutters of Cienfuegos, USNIP, Mar 1931, pg 353*
[28] *Travel voucher, dated May 21, 1898, Bandholtz papers UMICH*

instrumental in recruiting the regiment in the former Indian Territories of the Western United States. Roosevelt resigned his position with the Navy to serve with this unit, under the command of Colonel Leonard Wood. However, Wood was soon placed in command of a Cavalry Brigade, and Roosevelt, who had been his assistant, assumed the leadership position.

Tampa was just one of several staging areas for an invasion force. However, it was not equipped to handle such an influx of men and equipment. Initially, Tampa authorities were notified there would be seven regiments of Infantry arriving, which would need an encampment. These seven regiments were to be regular soldiers, transported from various posts around the country. While suitable sites were located, the numbers increased dramatically until the area became overwhelmed.

Infantry training in Tampa
Wehman Collection, Univ of South Florida

Transporting a single regiment, the $5^{th}$ US Infantry, shipping in from New Orleans, took a train of 53 cars to move the men, horses, mules, and supply wagons. From April through August, 13,239 railroad cars filled with supplies were received and unloaded in Tampa. Volunteer regiments were also arriving, and these came in lacking clothing, equipment, and in at least one case ($32^{nd}$ Michigan Volunteer Infantry) with no weapons. It was soon to the point, whereby the soldiers outnumbered the local citizenry by a great margin.

Along with these citizen soldiers came discipline problems, putting a strain on local authorities. The troop build-ups saw an increase in saloons, gambling establishments and houses of prostitution, along with criminal elements determined to relieve the troops of their pay.

One infantry regiment, the famous New York $69^{th}$ "Fighting Irish," made up primarily of Irish Catholics, learned there was a Catholic Convent located in Tampa. Begging for mercy, these enterprising gentlemen concocted a story of being under-fed, and unpaid. The nuns began fixing meals, on a regular basis, for these poor destitute soldiers. That is, until the regimental commander came forward announcing to the nuns they had been taken in. The soldiers were being paid an allowance for food, which they were pocketing because of the charitable acts of the sisters.[29]

Regular troops were accustomed to living in the open, and handling the weather, but the Volunteers were not so fortunate. The uniform of the day consisted of cowhide leather boots, flannel shirts, and woolen trousers, not conducive to tropical temperatures in Florida, nor Cuba. Food and supplies were arriving at a slower rate than troops with the result of poor diet and little war preparation. Some regiments received no rations for days at a time. General William Shafter,[30] is quoted, "The main cause for delay has been the fact that great stores had been rushed in promiscuously; and with no facilities to handle or store them. The last ten miles before reaching the wharf is a single track and very narrow space to work. The capacity of this place is greatly excceded." However, the troops had to first get to Cuba. On May 30, 1898, a message was sent to General

---

[29] *The Role of Florida in the Spanish-American War, 1898,"* by William J. Schellings, doctoral dissertation, *University of Florida*
[30] *Major General William Rufus Shafter (1835-1906), Michigan native, Commander of $5^{th}$ Army Corps in Cuba*

Shafter, Commander of the invasion force, by Nelson Miles, General Commanding the Army, which read: *"You are directed to take your command on transports, proceed under convoy of the Navy to the vicinity of Santiago de Cuba, land your force at such place east or west of that point as your judgment may dictate, under the protection of the Navy to capture or destroy the garrison there, and with the aid of the Navy capture or destroy the Spanish fleet now reported to be in the Santiago Harbor. When will you sail?"*[31]

While military expeditions by sea date back to ancient times, America was relatively inexperienced to this type operation. During the War for Independence, in 1775, Continental Army Troops were transported by barge, on rivers in Canada, in an ill-fated attempt to capture Quebec, and in 1832 a small contingent of Marines were landed in Sumatra in a punitive expedition.[32] This was in retaliation for a Malay attack on an American trading vessel, "The Friendship." Later would come the landing on March 9, 1847, below Vera Cruz, Mexico, during the Mexican-American War, and then an amphibious invasion of Korea during 1871. This latter operation resulted after the Korean burning of an American trading sloop "General Sherman," and the killing of all onboard, many of whom were missionaries. A landing force of 10 Infantry Companies, 2 Artillery Batteries, supported by Pioneers and Medical personnel, totaling 651 men went ashore in launches. Supported by the gunships Palos and Monocacy, some forts in the landing area were destroyed, and troops skirmished with Korean troops. Like the excursion into Sumatra,[33] this was a punitive expedition; no land was occupied, the force was returned to their ships, and the Task Force left Korea.[34]

---

[31] *A Leap to Arms*, by Jack Cameron. Dierks, J. B. Lippincott Co., New York, pg 70
[32] *The Korean Expedition of 1871*, USNIP, Feb 1948, pg 197
[33] *The Attack on Quallah-Battoo*, USNIP, July 1953, pgs 767-771
[34] *Korean Life and Culture*, U. of Maryland-Far East Division, Seoul, Korea. During 1964, the author was taught that the sinking of the

Cuba would be the next American effort at waging war on foreign soil, where amphibious landings were required. It would also pit American troops against a well armed Spanish Military. The Spaniards were equipped with modern Mauser rifles and Krupp cannons, using smokeless powder, while most of the US Volunteers were armed with the US Springfield Rifle, a single shot breechloader, and antiquated field guns using black powder cartridges. Some regular troops did have the newer Krag Rifle, Model of 1896, which had a five shot magazine, and a smokeless cartridge. However, even this weapon was vastly inferior to the Mauser. In most cases, therefore, every time an American fired a weapon, the telltale white smoke would identify his position. Even the US Gatling guns fired black powder cartridges.

The climate in Cuba was tropical, warm and moist, with sudden torrential downpours. The terrain was jungle like, difficult for the movement of troops and their equipment. Supply wagons, artillery, and Gatling carriages, would have a difficult time maneuvering.

In a totally separate landing, on June 10th, 1898, members of the all-black 10th Cavalry, left the U.S.S. Florida, and landed at Tayabacoa, to make contact with Cuban nationalist fighters. Their intention was to have the Cuban leaders coordinate their attacks against the Spaniards during the upcoming invasion. The landing site, however, was close to a Spanish garrison, and after a brief firefight, the landing party evacuated the beach. The Spaniards captured sixteen wounded men, who had been left behind. A rescue force, all volunteer, was dispatched from the "Florida," and consisted of just four men, Privates George Henry Wanton, Dennis Bell, Fitz Lee, and William Thomkins. These four were able to land unnoticed onto the beach and melt into the night.

---

*Sherman was instrumental in bringing Christianity to Korea, through Bibles found in the ruins of the ship*

Making their way to the fort, they crept inside and surprised the few Spaniards, who were guarding the prisoners in a stockade. They had one thing in mind, getting these men back the boats safely, then back to the ships, without stirring the Spanish garrison. The walking wounded were able to help, by carrying the more seriously wounded, and by stealth were able to navigate in the warm and humid darkness to where the boats were beached. Quietly loading the boats, they pushed away from shore, going as far as they could before using the oars. Jubilant troopers on the ships welcomed the adventurers back, and saw to it that the former captives were taken care of. The volunteers were awarded Medals of Honor[35] on June 23$^{rd}$, 1899, becoming the first four black men to be so honored for this war.

Meanwhile, back in Tampa, the loading of 25,000 troops and their equipment, onto a conglomeration of chartered steamers proved a nightmare. These boats had to be refitted for troop transport, with troops milling around not knowing where or when to board. The Chief Surgeon 5$^{th}$ Army Corps, Lieutenant Colonel Benjamin F. Pope,[36] stated, "The ships had strands of rough lumber bunks, usually three tiers high, often four, built into the holds and lower and main decks. The packing of these bunks so close that there was hardly room to pass between them, while in too many instances with the closure of the hatches, light and air could be wholly excluded and suffocation quickly result."

The Army's supplies were still sealed aboard 300 railway boxcars scattered around the Tampa area. Several days passed while confusion reigned, and more troops and supplies were arriving daily. As the ships started to load, many were seized by troop commanders, rather than being assigned by manifest. The single rail line, to dockside, was constantly filled to capacity, while the cars were unloaded and stevedores loaded the cargo onto the proper vessels.

---

[35] *Medal of Honor Recipients, US Army Center for Military History*
[36] *LTC Benjamin Franklin Pope, USA Medical Officer, (d. Feb 14, 1902)*

Lieutenant Colonel Theodore Roosevelt loaded the "Rough Riders," after he had commandeered the ship "Yucatan" which had been consigned to the 2$^{nd}$ Infantry and 71$^{st}$ NY Volunteer Infantry. He refused to disembark, so those troops had to find other ships to board. It turned out that the ships would not hold all 25,000 troops, so only about 18,000 were loaded.[37]

Troops awaiting loading in Tampa
Hampton Dunn Collection, Univ. of South Florida

The loading of troops faced an unexpected problem, when white soldiers refused to be billeted with colored troops. With a segregated Army, provisions had to be made for these concerns. Brothers-in-Arms they may have been, but racial bias reared its ugly head. In the upcoming battles discrimination would show up again and again.

Finally, at 3:30 AM, June 14, the convoy left Tampa. The breeze caused by the ships forward movement, caused a little

---

[37] *A Leap to Arms*, pg 72, 73

relief during those hot June days, but this was countered by the seasickness caused by the constant movement of the ships. There were 35 transports, 4 tenders, 1 hospital ship, and 14 naval escort vessels. It again took several days to sail the short distance to where the landings were to take place. It was not until seven days later that the convoy was in Cuban waters off Santiago. By this time, rations and supplies had been depleted, the troops were very anxious to get ashore.

The weather was bright and sunny, and the water relatively calm. The ships were in the deep blue waters, but as the landing boats neared shore, the color changed to aquamarine. Serene, but still very dangerous with so many troops being landed. The clear water was deceiving, allowing soldiers to think they were in shallow water, while it was still very deep.

Disembarking the soldiers along the beaches of Cuba was problematic. The landing was not completed until days later. Men could ride the small boats into the surf, climb over the sides, and make it to land. As the boats came close to the beach, men would position themselves to get off. One boat overturned, two troopers of the 10$^{th}$ Cavalry went into the water. Frantic cries for help went out, men grasped for their fallen comrades, sailors dove in for the rescue. Sadly, the two sank into the warm salty water. The equipment the men were wearing pulled them under, efforts to help them continued, but failed. Neptune's minions had claimed two brave men on the doorstep of their great adventure. An after action report is cruel in its simplicity, "It was recorded, "A boat has been overturned. Men of the 10$^{th}$ Cavalry tied in blanket rolls and weighted cartridge belts were in the water. It is horrible to think of them clasped in the arms of their heavy accouterments. Wild excitement reigned on the pierhead, lines were flung, men tried to reach down to the water; overboard from launches and cutters went blue-jackets, gallant blue-jackets, while over that hub-hub the sound of the same rasping voice screamed senselessly to do this, to do that. Well, two of them were gone - killed on the doorstep of

Cuba, drowned a moment before they could set on that island which had been the subject of their soldierly dreams."[38]

The landing went on, and companies of soldiers were marched off the beach, to make room for additional boats to land. Assembly areas were established to gather stragglers and get them to their respective units. The men were able to see their first island natives, and the conditions in which they lived. It was a great relief to get away from the cramped conditions of life on the transports, and walking got the kinks out of the legs.

Meanwhile, horses for the officers and cavalry were sometimes forced overboard and encouraged to swim for shore. Buglers were landed on the beach and played bugle calls, hoping to attract the horses into swimming towards land. Several swam the wrong way and drowned. Fortunately, the landing at Daiquiri went unopposed by Spanish troops. General Garcia's irregulars were keeping the Spaniards busy inland. Heavier equipment was brought ashore at available loading docks in the immediate and neighboring areas.[39]

From the assembly areas, the units marched to their assigned bivouac areas, miles from the beach. Tramping through dense vegetation, with frequent tropical downpours, the troops were hot, wet and quickly tired. Their woolen uniforms soaked up moisture like a sponge. Missed trails frequently caused confusion as the troops had to reverse the march and get back on the right track. Some fortunate units had local Cuban guides to assist in finding their way. Several days of marching were required to get all of the units close to where they would launch their first attack against the fortified Spanish positions.

---

[38] *Soldiers and Patriots, Buffalo Soldiers and Afro-Cubans in Tampa, 1898*, Brent R. Weisman, July 1999, USF Anthropology Dept.
[39] *A Splendid Little War, Online History of the Spanish-American War*

In a letter home, written before the El Caney Battle, Corporal T. H. Dunn,[40] of Company B, 7th US Infantry, writes, "I tell you everything is in a fearful state here. I did not think that an island as near our country had so many starving and destitute people and it is high time this state of things is stopped and the poor Cubans made free. If I am fortunate enough to pull through safe, I will be very glad but if it be my fate to get killed or die from sickness I believe I will have died for a good deed."

As they neared the positions where they were to launch the attack, the troops were told to be quiet, but you could hear the sound of men marching, and their equipment was rattling in the night. Horses of the officers, and troops in the front ranks, churned up the trail so that those following were slogging through mud. The soldiers could feel the mud trying to suck the boots off their feet as they marched. The night air was warm and humid, men complaining about their discomfit. Trails were narrow, more like animal paths, and the dew-covered vegetation soon had the trousers of the soldiers soaked. Palmetto and other similar plants had sharp, razor like edges, their points were like bayonets. Frequent stops were necessary for the stragglers to catch up to the column.

Serious business loomed ahead, everyone was wondering how he would behave in his first battle. Silence was the key to keeping the Spaniards unaware of American positions. Upon arrival at the jump off position, orders were passed; no fires or open lights of any kind. The men were able to rest for a while, but few slept. Artillery batteries worked in the dark to get their guns into position, but would have to wait until light to sight them in. Observation balloons would be raised to pinpoint enemy positions and adjust the cannon fire.

---

[40] *A letter from Thomas Henry Dunn, Spanish American War Centennial Website*

On July 1st, at El Caney, just 550 Spanish soldiers under General Joaquín Vara del Rey[41] were instructed to hold the northwest flank of Santiago against an American advance. Battle hardened troops from the "Constitution" regiment, supported by elements of the "Asia" and "Cuba" regiments, defended their fortified positions. They had previously faced severe fighting against the insurgent Cubans, who were struggling for independence from Spain.

The American assault began at dawn, as the artillery opened fire. The earth trembled as the explosive shells landed in and around the Spanish positions. Huge sections of earth were tossed every which way as the defenders tried to find cover. Whistles screeched and bugles blared, signaling for the American troops to advance. They moved forward, in skirmish lines; the uphill climb was over ground of various types, from plowed fields, to rock strewn areas of dense brush, often with barbed wire entanglements. It was not a "walk in the park" by any stretch of the imagination. The assault force, and the Spanish defenders, increased their volume of rifle fire. Soldiers could be seen dropping to the ground; some were falling to get away from the gunfire, but others were suffering with wounds. Orders could be heard prompting the men to continue on. A depression, or sunken road, offered a place of safety for several soldiers of the 7th Infantry. The exhausted troops were reluctant to advance through the storm of enemy fire. Officers were frantically trying to get them up and moving forward again.

Despite the lack of machine guns and artillery, and being denied promised reinforcements, General Vara del Rey and his soldiers held over eight thousand Americans from their position for nearly twelve hours, preventing them from sweeping through and overwhelming the defenders of San

---

[41] *Joaquín Vara del Rey y Rubio (1840 – July 1, 1898) Spanish soldier and general. He was killed leading the stubborn defense of El Caney against a massively superior American army during the Spanish-American War.*

Juan Hill. It had been thought that Lawton's Second Division would take El Caney in a short time, and move on to San Juan Hill. The assault division consisted of the 7$^{th}$, 12$^{th}$, and 17$^{th}$ Infantry Regiments, with Miles' Brigade in reserve.

With bullets and shells flying through the air, the noise was deafening; this in addition to the cries of the wounded. The smell of death, the acrid odors from the shellfire, combined with the blood lost by those wounded and killed, was disconcerting to many. To the rear of the American lines, the field guns were belching out great clouds of smoke, and the Gatling guns kept up a staccato rhythm. Early in the fight, Major Augustus W. Corliss,[42] 7$^{th}$ Infantry Regimental Adjutant, was wounded and removed from the field of battle. Harry Bandholtz was ordered to fill the post, which he performed with great bravery. He wanted to perform well, knowing many of the soldiers in his regiment were much more experienced in warfare. A few of the "old-timers" saw skirmishes during the Indian Wars. Others, of foreign birth, had experienced battles with the armies of their native lands. In a letter written at the time, Captain George S. Young, Harry's immediate supervisor wrote, "his (Bandholtz) conduct on that occasion was conspicuous for bravery and fearlessly exposing himself under heavy fire."[43] For his actions on this day, Harry was brevetted a Captain. Years later, he would be recognized for his valor, through the award of a Silver Star Citation. Unfortunately this award was made posthumously. Two other 7$^{TH}$ Infantry soldiers, Sergeant Major Samuel W. Shaffer, and Corporal Frank P. McMurphy received the Distinguished Service Cross.

A fellow officer in the 7$^{th}$ Infantry, Captain George Wilcox McIver, Company B, writes in his memoirs that the 7$^{th}$ Infantry led the movement to El Caney. The American Battle Line advanced across open ground, while the Spanish

---

[42] *Gen. Augustus W. Corliss. (1837-1908) native of Maine*
[43] *A Biography-Harry Hill Bandholtz 1864-1925, Grafton H. Cook II, page 25-36, unpublished*

defenders were concealed in houses, behind walls, in blockhouses, and a stone fort called El Viso. Casualties were heavy, but elements of the 12$^{th}$ Infantry, were able to capture the stone fort. With its capture the Spanish firing seemed to subside.[44]

However, the New York Times, on July 18, 1898, in an article entitled "Battle of El Caney," credits the 25$^{th}$ Infantry Regiment, a negro unit, of actually capturing the stone fort, describing in some detail the heroics of the soldiers of that regiment. The 12$^{th}$ Infantry is also mentioned as taking part in that particular action.[45]

The story relates Colonel Miles' Brigade, being held as reserve, was ordered forward, with the 4$^{th}$ and 25$^{th}$ Infantry Regiments in the lead. The 4$^{th}$ was soon under extreme fire, and pinned down. Sending forward reserve companies to protect their flank, the 25$^{th}$ continued the advance. These fresh troops passed through the battle weary 7$^{th}$ and 12$^{th}$ Regiments, and stormed forward. The men of the 25$^{th}$, followed by several companies of the 4$^{th}$ and 12$^{th}$, forced their way through the Spanish lines, then rushed into the fort. The Spaniards fled in disarray, and the battle ended shortly thereafter.

The 25th Infantry Regiment was organized at Jackson Barracks, Louisiana in April 1868 from African American recruits who had served in the US Army during the Civil War. Colored Regiments were typically and almost without exceptions officered entirely by white officers, however the non-commissioned officers were drawn from the ranks. It is an accepted fact that the long serving sergeants of the black regiments were professional soldiers of the highest quality.

To this day the 12th is credited with capturing the blockhouse, even making it part of their unit insignia. This

---

[44] *A Life of Duty-The Autobiography of George Wilcox McIver 1858-1947, James Dembo. Editor, The History Press 2006,*
[45] *Battle of El Caney," New York Times, July 18, 1898*

was done even under official protest from Lieutenant Colonel A. S. Daggett, the commander of the 25th at the Battle of El Caney.[46] However, the Fortress of Al Caney is also depicted on the unit insignia of the 25th.

Sergeant Major Frank Pullen, of the 25th, recalled the events of the day, "Finally, late in the afternoon, our brave Lieutenant Kinnison said to another officer: "We cannot take the trenches without charging them." Just as he was about to give the order for the bugler to sound "the charge," he was wounded and carried to the rear. The men were then fighting like demons. Without a word of command, though led by that gallant and intrepid Second Lieutenant James A. Moss, 25th Infantry, some one gave a yell and the 25th Infantry was off, alone to the charge. The 4th U.S. Infantry, fighting on the left, halted when those dusky heroes made the dash with a yell that would have done credit to a Comanche Indian. No one knows who started the charge; one thing is certain, at the time it was made excitement was running high; each man was a captain for himself and fighting accordingly.

It has been reported that the 12th U.S. Infantry made the charge, assisted by the 25th Infantry, but it is a recorded fact that the 25th Infantry fought the battle alone, the 12th Infantry coming up after the firing had nearly ceased. Private T. C. Butler, Company H, 25th Infantry, was the first man to enter the blockhouse at El Caney, and took possession of the Spanish flag for his regiment. An officer of the 12th Infantry came up while Butler was in the house and ordered him to give up the flag, which he was compelled to do, but not until he had torn a piece off the flag to substantiate his report to his Colonel of the injustice which had been done to him. Thus, by using the authority given him by his shoulder-straps, this officer took for his regiment that which had been

---

[46] *Buffalo Soldier Regiment-History of the 25th Infantry Regiment, by John H. Nankivell, U. of Nebraska Press, 2001*

won by the hearts' blood of some of the bravest, though black, soldiers of Shafter's army." [47]

The American casualty list was staggering: over 80 dead and 350 wounded. In this action, the 7$^{th}$ Infantry had one officer and 32 men killed, four officers and 95 men wounded. Three additional men were missing. Eleven of the wounded died later from the wounds received. The unit strength had been 850 men. Precise Spanish losses at El Caney are not known, but the Cuban irregulars also suffered heavily, 150 killed and wounded that day.[48]

In his diary,[49] a Spanish Naval Officer, who was a witness to the battle wrote: "The Americans, to tell the truth, fought that day showing a determination and courage that was really magnificent. The houses of El Caney, transformed by General Vara and his 520 men into fortresses, vomited out a rain of bullets over the enemy, who, in order of companies, with their chests as their only protection, tried fiercely to run over the village.

With the first line decimated, another one came to its replacement, and one after another; and those soldiers, seemed more like animated statues than human beings, if it is allowed to me to say; but they met heroes, and even with the houses riddled with bullet holes by artillery and rifle fire, and its streets obstructed by the wounded and dead bodies, El Caney became a true volcanoe vomitting (Sic) lava, and a place impossible to reach."

After burying the dead, and removing the prisoners, Lawton's Division marched towards the battle lines in front of the City of Santiago, arriving during the hours of darkness. The rest of the Army had fought the battles of San Juan and Kettle Hills, so the way to Santiago was clear. Here the troops were kept in reserve and the men were able to get

---

[47] *Ibid*
[48] *Spanish American Ear, by Daniel E. Brannen. Jr., Thompspn-Gale*
[49] *Tejeira Jose Muller, Combates y Capiulacion de Santiago, Madred, 1898*

some sleep. Although the 7th Infantry was constantly under enemy fire, they managed to avoid any additional casualties. As the reserve force, they were busily digging entrenchments and preparing to enter the battle for the City of Santiago.[50]

With the fighting over, General Shafter verbally issued an order, through Lieutenant Colonel Carpenter, dated July 13, 1898, to the effect that Harry would be relieved of his duties in order to accept the commission as Major in the newly formed 35th Michigan Infantry Regiment.[51]

Three days later, after the fall of Santiago, the Spaniard and American commanders agreed to surrender terms, the formal surrender taking place on July 17th. Fighting was over in Cuba, but the Spanish-American War was ongoing in Puerto Rico and the Philippines.

Relieved of his position, Harry was freed to return to the United States where he accepted a volunteer commission with the Michigan Volunteer Infantry, which he had declined in Tampa unless allowed to first finish the campaign upon which his regular regiment was about to enter.

On his way home, all of Harry's personal belongings were lost at sea. Upon arrival in Tampa, he was placed in quarantine for five days, before being allowed to travel to see May and Cleveland, in Chicago. Before reporting for his new assignment at Island Lake, Michigan, Harry stopped in Constantine to visit his mother, and then at Kalamazoo where he purchased new uniforms and equipment. On August 6th, Major Harry Bandholtz was sworn into the 35th Michigan Infantry Regiment.[52]

---

[50] *A Biography Harry Hill Bandholtz 1864-1925, Grafton H. Cook II*
[51] *Ibid*
[52] *Ibid*

# Chapter Five

# TROUBLE IN AUGUSTA, GEORGIA

Major H. H. Bandholtz, 35th Michigan V.I. (1898)
Bandholtz papers, UMICH

Upon his return from Cuba, Harry Bandholtz was commissioned Major of the 35th Michigan Volunteer Infantry,[53] effective July 25, 1898. The 35th became a part of the 1st Division, 2nd Army Corps, and was transferred to Camp McKenzie, close to Augusta, Georgia to prepare for service in the war. He later received the following orders: *"Headquarters 1st Division, 2nd Army Corps, Camp McKenzie, Ga. 12-2-1898, Special Orders 183. The appointment of Major Harry H. Bandholtz, 35th Michigan V.I., as Provost Marshal of the Division is hereby continued until further orders. By command of BG Corbin."* This is the first document found of Provost Marshal duties assigned to Major Bandholtz.[54]

---

[53] *Officers Muster In Roll, Jul 25, 1898, Bandholtz papers*
[54] *Bandholtz Papers, UMICH*

On November 15, 1898, three months after the armistice went into effect but still a month before the end of the war, the 15th Minnesota was ordered on to Camp McKenzie where it joined with the 35$^{th}$ Michigan, and other units of the division. This Camp was organized as a winter camp for the Headquarters of the 2nd Army Corps, and two brigades of the First Division. The 15$^{th}$ Minnesota was known as "the sickest regiment in the Army," because of all the illnesses occurring within that unit, beginning shortly after the unit was formed near Minneapolis. Typhoid fever had run through the troops like wildfire.

There were four companies - F, K, M, and Nobles County's H, that were notably hard-hit. The four were ordered to relocate and they were separated from the remainder of the regiment by a distance of 100 yards. Lime was spread over the areas they had vacated. Company H suffered the most. The unit consisted of four commissioned officers and 105 enlisted men. Of these, only eight never answered sick call. There were three who died.[55]

On February 4, 1899, a private, Dennis O'Connell, of Company F, accompanied by his brother and two other companions, was drinking in a saloon in the Augusta area. As the drinking went on, the men were noisy, using profane and vulgar language in the presence of the wife of saloonkeeper, C. Brown Hadley. He warned the men about their language and a shouting match ensued. It was then that Brown Hadley produced a handgun and shot O'Connell, the bullet striking the victim's chest, killing him. At the time, O'Connell was just 24 years of age. After the shooting, Hadley ran outside, mounted his horse and rode away. He surrendered to authorities sometime later, away from the scene of the shooting.[56]

---

[55] *The Odyssey of the 15$^{th}$ Minnesota, the Spanish American War Centennial Website*
[56] *Minnesota Soldiers Riotous, Atlanta Constitution, Feb 9, 1899*

O'Connell was well respected within his unit, his friends were furious when the news from Augusta arrived. A number of the soldiers met to determine what should be done. An estimated 300 men gathered in front of the tent of their commander, Colonel Harry A. Leonhaeuser, demanding he speak with them about the incident. He declined to do so, but received a few representatives and gave them assurances that he would do everything within his power to bring the murderer to justice.

Later in the evening, approximately 150 soldiers broke out of camp heading for Augusta. They were enraged and were seeking revenge for the death of O'Connell. A lieutenant from their unit managed to overtake them, calm them down and got them to return to camp.

Early the following morning, word reached camp that Brown Hadley, the shooter of O'Connell, had been captured and was being prepared for transport to Atlanta. Less than an hour later, soldiers, being led by Private Peter Foley, also of Company F, overpowered the few officers and NCOs guarding the ammunition storehouse. Breaking open the ammunition crates, with pickaxes, they armed themselves and started on the road to Augusta. Colonel Leonhaeuser tried to stop the mutineers, but a group of 70 continued with the march.[57]

Major Bandholtz, Division Provost Marshal, had been on alert from the day before, because of the unrest. He had taken the precaution of placing on standby six troops of cavalry, in addition to a large contingent of his Provost Guard.[58] The Provost Guard was dispatched and was able to turn most of the riotous troops around, returning them to camp under guard. The ringleaders were identified and put into shackles.[59]

---

[57] G.O. 127, Hqs., Dept of Army, Court of Inquiry, dated July 8, 1890
[58] Atlanta Constitution, Feb 6, 1899
[59] Minnesota in the Spanish-American War and Philippine Insurrection, published by Minnesota War Commission

Elements of the Provost Guard, Troop A of the cavalry, and troopers of the 35$^{th}$ Michigan, had also been dispatched to Augusta where they rounded up all soldiers and removed them from the city. Some were left guarding the home of C. Brown Hadley, which was reportedly a target of the mutineers. In the meantime, Hadley had been transported to Atlanta and placed in the Fulton County Jail, pending trial.

Camp McKenzie was placed on "lock-down," the Commanding General, MG Samuel Sumner initiated an embargo, forbidding troops from visiting Augusta. A week later, a delegation from Augusta visited the camp pleading that the soldiers be allowed to come into town. They convinced General Sumner of their sincerity and the embargo was lifted.[60]

Harry Bandholtz is credited with calming the near riot of troops from this Minnesota Regiment, as is shown in a letter of commendation from the Division Commander, MG Samuel S. Sumner, dated Oct 10, 1899: "Lt. H. H. Bandholtz, 7$^{th}$ U.S. Infantry,

*Dear Sir: It affords me much pleasure to certify to the energetic and efficient manner in which you performed the duty of Provost Marshal at Augusta, Ga., last winter. That you were selected for that responsible position, and kept on such detail during the entire time you remained in Augusta, is good evidence of the manner in which you performed the duty. The quiet and good order that prevailed generally in camp and in the city, was due in a great measure to your energy and good judgment. I wish particularly to certify the able manner in which you appreciated the unfortunate outbreak of the 15$^{th}$ Minn. Regiment. Your instant call on the Cavalry, and disposition of the Provost Guard, prevented what might have grown into a serious outbreak. As the Commanding Officer of the Division, I am very glad to send you this acknowledgement of your service under me."*[61] This

---

[60] *Augusta Chronicle Newspaper, Thursday, February 9 1899*
[61] *Letter of Appreciation, Bandholtz papers*

letter was sent after Harry had left volunteer service, and rejoined the 7th Infantry.

As a result of this unfortunate incident, General Courts Martial, at Division Headquarters, tried nine of the instigators. Eight of these were found guilty, sentenced to dishonorable discharge, forfeiture of all pay and allowances, and confinement for periods ranging from six months to six years. Those sentenced to imprisonment were transferred to St Francis Barracks, St Augustine, Florida, where they were incarcerated.[62]

On March 27, 1899, eight months after the troops began their pointless and ill-fated tour of duty, the 15th Minnesota Volunteer Infantry was mustered out of the federal service. The men were free to return home.[63] During the travel back from Georgia, several former members of the regiment were involved in incidents, but since they had been released these incidents were of more concern to civilian authorities.

In July 1899, the 35th Michigan was released from active duty, Harry Bandholtz again returned to his regiment. Those with whom he served sent letters and commendations for the good fellowship and professional behavior during their months together. His service as Division Provost Marshal gave him a background experience that would serve him well in the years to follow.

Harry reverted to his regular army rank of First Lieutenant but was soon promoted to Captain. Most likely, because of his ability to speak the Spanish language, he was returned to Cuba where he commanded Sagua La Grande District and supervised the free elections there. He remained in Cuba for five months, and then was ordered to the Philippine Islands.

---

[62] *Minnesota in the Spanish-American War*
[63] *The Odyssey of the 15th Minnesota*

## Chapter Six
## THE PHILIPPINES

At the end of the Spanish-American War, the opposing countries, the United States and Spain, met in Paris to negotiate peace. The commissioners began their talks on October 10, 1898, the resulting treaty was signed on December 10th. The outcome of the treaty was that Cuba would gain her independence from Spain, Puerto Rico and Guam would be ceded to the United States, the victorious United States would be allowed to purchase the Philippine Islands from Spain, for twenty million dollars.

Rather than an occupier, the United States thought of herself as a benefactor. Removing the Spanish was an initial step, and a process of building a new government began; the aim being to take an oppressed people and introduce them to an improved American style civilization. However, many Filipinos saw the Americans as another tyrannical overseer, one that must be fought until independence could be achieved. Upon his return to the Philippines, from Hong Kong, Aguinaldo had declared Independence for the Philippines.

What was received for the twenty million dollars was an archipelago comprised of thousands of islands spread across the western Pacific. It was a primitive land with little or no electrification outside of the major cities. Transportation on land was restricted to animal driven carts or wagons, and inter-island travel was by boat.

American military forces were transported to the islands to protect America's interests. Tension between the Americans and the Filipinos grew so great that it was easy to precipitate a war. On the night of February 4, 1899, an American sentry, Private William W. Grayson, with another soldier, encountered three armed Filipinos on a bridge in San Juan del Monte near Manila.[64] The war started by this incident would last another 16 years.

By permission, Military Police Museum

In July 1900, Harry was transferred to the Philippines, where he served for the next 13 years. Upon his arrival, the Philippine Islands were a country in turmoil. The Americans had merely replaced the Spaniards as the "oppressor." Insurgent armies were disturbing the general populace, and Captain Bandholtz's mission was to help establish peace.

This was a troublesome task. The insurgent tribes would attack and then disappear into the jungle. Pursuit was difficult, and the paths through the tall grasses were less than friendly. As an army patrol maneuvered through the thick brush, the enemy could be watching from their hiding places close by. Primitive traps were set along the faintest of trails, and triggered by the movement of the men. Often the troops would find themselves suddenly surrounded by ferocious

---

[64] *Aguinaldo: A Narrative of Filipino Ambitions*, E. Wildman 1901, Norwood Press, Norwood, MA

fighters, wielding spears and various types of sharp cutting or chopping instruments, the entire patrol would be brutally cut down. Those captured, would suffer the most horrible of tortures before they were freed by death from the agonizing pain.

Other tribes in the islands practiced the same type ambushes, and each carried their own type of weapons. Mostly cutting tools, the various tribes would use the bolo, a kris (dagger or sword length blade), barong (similar to the bolo), and in Moro areas, the Kampilan sword.

Harry's first duties in the islands were with the $2^{nd}$ Infantry, Central Luzon, and on the island of Marinduque. In April of 1901, he took one other officer, Lieutenant Campbell King, and they walked unarmed, through the wilderness, until reaching the camp of insurgent leader Colonel Maximo Abad.

Maximo Abad on his way to surrender, accompanied by Harry Hill Bandholtz, Boac, Marinduque Island, Philippines, Apr. 1901, from the Bandholtz papers

As he walked through the jungle he planned what he would offer the insurgent leader, to assure him there was a better way to solve the problems of his people. In his convincing way, Harry impressed upon Abad that the best solution would be for that man's surrender. He walked out again, accompanied by Abad and his entire command.[65] He quickly gained a reputation of being sincere in his dealings with the Filipinos, and they found they were able to trust him.

It had only been seven months since Abad and his band ambushed and defeated an American force of 54 men of the 29th Infantry. Through gathering intelligence from guerilla fighters, Abad was able to track the movements of Captain Devereux Shields, and his men. He waited until he had an opportune time, and location, to completely encircle the American force. The resulting battle cost the beleaguered detachment four dead, and six wounded, all survivors being captured.

In June of 1901, Harry was sent to Tayabas Province (now Quezon Province). Within this Province, there is a holy place where the men have gone for worship for many generations. As part of the simple ritual of their services, they wore red sashes. In the early days, it had been the simple religion of a simple, childlike people called "Pulajans."

The group obtained their name from their distinctive dress, the word pula in Visayan, (language family in the central islands of the Philippines) meaning red. The tribe had been simple highlanders, cultivating the mountain clearings in peace. Without exception, the hill people of the Philippines are timid and peaceful, unless provoked.

Their own countrymen had forced these people into banditry. They had raised their crops of rice and hemp, carrying them on their shoulders to the sea settlements for sale or trade. The Pulajan is a retiring creature, not too well understood by his sophisticated cousins of the cities. His religion had no complicated ritual and is centered on nature. He knows little of the arts of commerce and finance. Too often the tribe became a victims of shrewd merchants.

---

[65] *Record of Harry Hill Bandholtz, Bandholtz Papers, UMICH*

The robbing tactics of the latter brought on retaliatory raids. As the movement grew in strength, it took on a tone of religious ritual and frenzy. It also came under the influence of unscrupulous native leaders who saw in the hill people agents for their own personal advancement. The areas of Samar and Leyte became filled with crusading "Popes" who were self appointed "Messiahs" and who soon impressed their influence upon the childlike mountaineers. The seeds sown by the "Popes" began to bear fruit, the Pulajans now became militant crusaders with a developed hatred to law and order, and a homicidal intent towards their own countrymen in the lowlands. Their red tribal costumes became adorned with white crosses, the raids grew into ferocious forays that were out of all proportion to the original grievances of these hill people.[66]

After only one month in Tayabas Province, Harry was again able to enter into an insurgent camp, that of Colonel Mariano Castillo, where he received the surrender of the Colonel, and took possession of prisoners and 200 rifles. Both of the incidents, involving the surrender of Abad and Castillo, took place after negotiations with the leaders, through normal channels had broken down.

Following one such incursion into the "bush," Harry writes, "In traveling through the islands I have often wondered how it would feel to be captured by Pulajanes. Now that I have realized this ambition, I have at least one illusion dispelled. I find that instead of the water-cure they administer the chow-cure; that instead of being a band of horribly ferocious, ugly looking, unwashed and filthy beings they are really a handsome intelligent and clean looking, and apparently frequently bathed collection of gentlemen. I also imagined they all wore their hair long, but in looking at "Papa Jaime" I see that I was mistaken. Taking everything into consideration I find that being captured by the Pulajanes instead of being a catastrophe will be an unforgettable happy event."

---

[66] *Jungle Patrol*, Chapter 6

For those insurgents who were not willing to surrender their arms, the penalties were often severe. Several of the leaders of the more brutal groups were tried, and upon conviction, were ordered hanged. On at least one occasion, Harry was again assigned duties as Provost Marshal. However, on this occasion his responsibilities were the handling of the execution of two insurgent leaders. His orders read:

Execution, Bandholtz Papers, UMICH

"*Lucena, Tayabas Province, Luzon, P.I. October $1^{st}$, 1901, General Orders No. 18. In accordance with sentence of Military commission published in General Orders No. 24d, dated Headquarters Division of the Philippines, Manila, P.I., September $2^{nd}$ 1901, and instructions from Headquarters Department of Southern Luzon, native prisoners Leoncio Tabordan and Leonudo Macalaguin will be executed at this station October $11^{th}$, 1901, at 10 o'clock AM, or as near that hour as practicable. The execution will be public and the scaffold erected on the open space west of the Church in the Plaza of Lucena.*

*The troops of the command will be formed on the North and South sides of the scaffold in light marching order. The guard on the East side. The West side of the scaffold will be guarded by sentinels to prevent the approach of any unauthorized persons nearer the scaffold than the line of wall. The bodies of the executed persons will be turned over to the relatives or friends for burial upon application, otherwise will be buried by Military authorities.*

*Captain H. H. Bandholtz, Quartermaster $2^{nd}$ Infantry, is appointed Provost Marshal for this date and will perfect and have charge of all details. Captain Arthur Jordan, Assistant Surgeon, U. S. Vols. will report to Captain Bandholtz to make necessary examination and death certificate.*

*By order of Colonel Roberts:*

*/s/ Geo. C. Marlin, $1^{st}$ Lieut. & Batt Adjt. $2^{nd}$ Inft, Adjutant.*"[67]

During the American takeover of the Philippines from Spain in 1898, the district of El Principe, to which Casiguran, Mission of Dipaculao, and Mission of San Jose de Casignan belonged were disestablished and incorporated into the province of Tayabas by the first American Military Governor, Colonel Cornelius Gardener.

To establish a civilian government, the Taft Commission, was appointed by President McKinley on March 16, 1900, led by William Howard Taft, who as the first civilian governor, outlined a comprehensive development plan that he described as "the Philippines for the Filipinos . . . that every measure, whether in the form of a law or an executive order, before its adoption, should be weighed in the light of this question: Does it make for the welfare of the Filipino people, or does it not?" The plan was aimed at broadening a representative government but also expanding a system of free public elementary education. Filipinos were enthused, interpreting Taft's directives as leading to a much-desired independence. In July 1901 a Philippine Constabulary was

---

[67] *G.O. 18, Oct 1, 1901, Bandholtz papers*

organized as the national police force to control criminal activity and deal with the remaining insurgent groups. Military rule was ended on July 4, 1901, the Constabulary gradually took over from United States army units the responsibility for suppressing guerrilla and bandit activities.[68]

Later the Taft Commission proceeded with plans to hold a general election, rather than permit the provinces to be returned to military rule. When the ballots of the municipal councilmen from all the towns were tallied, in Tayabas Province, the winner and new governor was none other than Captain Harry H. Bandholtz. He was the only American Army officer elected by the people of a province. This would indicate that he was accepted by the population and is a tribute to his accomplishments for them. On February 5, 1902, he wrote the following application to accept this position:

*"The Adjutant General,*
*Division of the Philippines, Manila, P.I.*

*Sir:*

*Having been elected, on the fourth instant, as Governor of Tayabas Province, and subject to confirmation by the Civil Commission, I have the honor to request that I be authorized to enter upon the duties of said office on March 3, 1902. My resignation as Regimental Quartermaster, $2^{nd}$ Infantry, to be submitted to take effect on same date in case of approval of this application.*

*This request is made because the people of this province do not feel as yet prepared to place themselves under the governorship of a native; because they feel that I possess certain especial qualifications in an ability to read, write and speak in the Spanish language to a moderate extent, and in a knowledge of their needs and customs; because they*

---

66Philippines: A Country Study. Washington: Ronald E. Dolan, ed, GPO for the Library of Congress, 1991.

*desire a governor that will work in absolute harmony with the military authorities; and because they realize that the Province cannot progress until the insurrection is effectually stamped out, knowing that my earnest and sincere efforts will be applied in that direction.*

*Very respectfully, Captain H. H. B., $2^{nd}$ Infantry.*"[69]

The application was approved, and the appointment confirmed by the Civil Commission. He served over one year as governor during that time Tayabas Province, the largest Christian Province in the islands, was completely pacified.

In Tayabas, Harry took Manuel Luis Quezon[70] under his wing and gave him his political start in that province, by helping him get elected an Assemblyman. Harry and Manuel Quezon were both very active members of the Masonic Order, and that may have been their initial contact. They remained friends for life, and Quezon later became his government's representative in Washington. In later years, his people would elect him as President of the Philippines. Re-elected for a second term, Quezon went into exile, in the United States, during the Japanese occupation of the Islands. He died in New York during his presidency.

---

[69] *Bandholtz papers, UMICH*

[70] *Manuel Luiz Quezon, (1878-1944), A young Manuel Quezon joined Aguinaldo's Army, and in a year rose from private to major, and fought the Americans. Advancing under a flag of truce he was told Aguinaldo had been taken and that the revolt was over. The Americans took him to Manila and showed him Aguinaldo in captivity and Quezon spent six months in jail. He was furious at the United States when the rebellion collapsed. Out of jail, Quezon was so angry that he refused to learn English. But he met an American officer, General Bandholtz, the first American he had ever known well, and discovered promptly that Americans were not Spaniards. Bandholtz said that Quezon must learn English and that he would pay Quezon, instead of vice versa, to take lessons from him!*

Regarding his term as Governor, Harry describes the progress of his province, in his annual report.[71] While things were improving in many areas, several problems still existed. One shortfall that seemed to concern him, was a lack of teachers; being only one per 300 students. Revenues were insufficient for repairing schools, never mind trying to build new ones. The war continued to cause shortages in farm animals, and laborers to work in the fields.

---

[71] *Report of the Provincial Governor of Tayabas, within the Report of the Philippine Commission to the Secretary of War, 1905, US Printing Office, Washington, dated 1906*

# Chapter Seven

## CONSTABULARY

Drawing by Cadet H. H. Bandholtz, U.S.M.A.

On July 4, 1901, the military regime in the Islands came to an end, and the government was officially delegated to a Philippine Civil Commission. Luke E. Wright held the position of Commissioner of Commerce and Police. President McKinley appointed Wright, a former officer in the Confederate Army, and a Tennessee lawyer, to the Taft Commission. Peace was the thing Mr. Wright desired above all else. It was he who proposed the establishment of the Philippine Constabulary, that materialized as the result of

Act 175, Philippine Commission, dated August 18, 1901.[72] He later served as Taft's replacement as Governor General of the Philippines, remaining in politics after his return to the United States.

*"An Insular Constabulary is hereby established under the general supervision of the Civil Governor for the purpose of better maintaining peace, law and order in the various Provinces of the Philippines, organized, officered and governed as herein set forth, which shall be known as the Philippines Constabulary."*[73]

It was hoped that a force of 6,000 native police, well split into detachments, would maintain a semblance of order. Officers for the constabulary were selected chiefly from American volunteers, recently mustered out, and from honorably discharged soldiers of the United States Army. Some few Filipinos, whose loyalty was above suspicion, were appointed to the lower grades. Regular officers of the United States Army were detailed to the higher administrative positions.

The many islands of the Philippines formed a number of provinces, and all were placed within five Constabulary Districts. The senior officer of the district was an Assistant Chief, answerable to the Chief of Constabulary. At the provincial level, a Senior Inspector was in charge. He, in turn, divided the province into sections under a company officer. Recruiting was normally done within the province where the companies were to operate.

With a force of Filipino police preparing to take the field, there remained the question of their armament. The Commanding General of the Philippine Division was convinced it would be unwise to arm the new force with rifles. On the other hand, those opposed to a Constabulary

---

[72] *Luke E. White (1846-1922), 2d Philippine Commissioner, US Secretary of War 1908-09*
[73] *Jungle Patrol – The Story of the Philippine Constabulary, by Vic Hurley, 1938 E. P. Dutton & Co., Inc.*

had to admit that such a force could not take the field with police clubs. Orders were hastily placed in America for 1,000 Winchester shotguns and a suitable quantity of brass shells. Also ordered were 5,000 Colt revolvers, caliber .45. The Winchester Arms Company advised that they had no stock of repeating shotguns and were unable to fill the order without great delay. Other equipment and ordnance supplies were similarly lacking, forcing the men into action without raincoats, sufficient shoes or underwear, and with very deficient weapons.[74] Weapons having a range over 100 yards were not allowed the Constabulary troops, so most went into the field with shotguns using black powder cartridges, and a few mismatched revolvers. The weapons they carried would be no match against the modern Mauser rifles which insurgent groups had captured from Spanish troops.

In 1903, Governor Bandholtz was relieved of his position in Tayabas and was appointed Colonel in the Philippine Constabulary, where he was given the command of the Second District of Southern Luzon. During his time in the Constabulary he would learn every aspect of police work.

Also during 1903, May Bandholtz arrived in the islands to join her husband. Their relationship had been strained by frequent separations, this causing discord in their household. With the constant operations taking him away from home, she started finding fault in everything he did, accusing him of infidelity on many occasions, and lack of attention on others. Their son Cleveland came to the islands with his uncle George, and visited with his parents for a couple of months. Father and son enjoyed this time together, exploring the jungles and having their encounters with animals, many of which had been domesticated enough to remain close to their quarters. Wild birds and monkeys seemed to always be around, scrounging for handouts of food. Harry had begun collecting various items used in the Philippines, namely articles of war, such as bows and arrows, spears, shields, and

---

[74] *The Jungle Patrol*

a great assortment of edged weapons. From time to time, he added the bamboo hats, woodcarvings, and some furnishings.

In one hundred days, the district went from one of constant turmoil to one of a pacified native population. Insurgent leader, General Simpson Ola had been active in this area for well over a year. In time, Ola became such an efficient predator that he was elevated to the command of the consolidated band. His depredations became such that three Assistant Chiefs of Constabulary unsuccessfully took the field against him. On September 25, 1903 General Simeon Ola personally surrendered unconditionally to Colonel Bandholtz. As those Albay campaigns had approached the end, Harry had gone into a town alone to accept the surrender of Ola and his men. He slept there, with his prisoners. We have a view then, of a new and concealed joviality in his nature.

He came back with his prisoners--a long file of them-- with Harry and Ola riding on the front seat of an escort wagon. Judge Carson, of the Court of First Instance, had been sent to Albay to try the prisoners. With Captain Higgins, Carson met the escort wagon and Harry hailed him joyfully. "I want to introduce you to a friend of mine, Judge," he shouted. "Let me present you to Simeon Ola."

During another Albay insurrection, May insisted on accompanying her husband on the operation. She and Harry were riding in a horse drawn wagon, when a front wheel broke, parts of it striking one of the ponies. The bolting horse caused the wagon to overturn. May injured her ankle while jumping clear of the carriage. As a result, she suffered a severe sprain and had to be off her foot in excess of two weeks. When the operation required more of his time than she liked, Harry had her sent back to their quarters by special boat.

On February 28, 1904, one hundred fifty men under Magno Revel, a lieutenant of the rebellious leader Toledo, attacked the Constabulary's barracks at Oas. The raid caused the desertion of twenty Constabulary troopers, the slaughter of many resisting, and the loss of forty-eight rifles. In another phase of this campaign, Colonel Bandholtz again went into an insurgent camp, unarmed, with only a native guide. As a result, Colonel Antonio Loamo surrendered, giving up seventy men and thirty rifles. So many of these surrenders are recorded, but there is no record of what Harry did or said to inspire these various leaders. His bravery often bordered on recklessness, but in every instance the results were the same. Even his one capture, at the hand of the "Pulajans" turned into a happy circumstance for him.

Constabulary Formation, Bandholtz Papers, UMICH

During the month of May, an exiled insurgent leader, Artemio Ricarte,[75] who had secretly been smuggled into the Philippines from Hong Kong, was captured. He was interviewed by Harry at Constabulary Headquarters, later tried and convicted of possessing firearms, and imprisoned. After serving a reduced sentence, for good behavior, Ricarte was allowed to return to Hong Kong. Early in his career, he had been designated General of a Division, in Aquinaldo's Army.

---

[75] *Artemio Ricarte, b Oct 20, 1866, insurgent leader against Spanish Rule, and later against the Americans. Exiled to live in Hong Kong*

On August 2, 1904, Harry and May Bandholtz sailed for home, on leave. They boarded the ship, S.S. Coptic, in Hong Kong for the trans-pacific crossing, arriving in San Francisco on August 29th. The ship's manifest states their destination as Chicago, and they had claimed nine pieces of luggage between them. Their visit coincided with the 1904 World's Fair, in St Louis, which had as its center-point the Philippine Campaign. To house the Fair, 1,500 buildings were used to display exhibits, with 75 miles of walk and roadways. Sixty-two nations provided exhibits, making the 1904 Fair the largest ever. The Philippine exhibits included full sized replicas of indigenous villages and living quarters, an encampment of the "Philippine Scouts," as well as the Philippine Constabulary. The Constabulary Band performed several times, the entire contingent numbered several hundred men. A museum was adorned with flags and banners, primitive and modern weapons used by, or captured from insurgent groups, articles of uniforms, saddles and tack, including a pair of silver mounted bridles, owned and used by Colonel Bandholtz. Harry had provided over 200 pieces of the items being displayed, for his contributions to the Philippine Exhibit, he received a "Grand Prize," in the War category.[76] When his leave ended, Harry and May returned to the Philippines on February 12, 1905.

Living the "good life" at home must have been a big change, from the reaction upon his return to the islands. Captain Higgins, who was adjutant at Lucena, remembers Colonel Bandholtz returning from a long leave in the United States. "He was as fat as butter; cheeks round and pink, and legs so plump that they bulged over his leggings. He was ready to start his Albay campaigns again, six months later, he sent for me. All his fat was gone--he was as skinny as a rail and as brown as an Indian. He had lived in the saddle for half a year but Albay was clean."

---

[76] *Report of the Philippine Exposition Board, St Louis 1904*

In his annual report, as Director, 2$^{nd}$ District of Constabulary, Harry criticized the continued use of the Springfield Model Carbines, for Constabulary. He writes, "Experience has amply demonstrated that single-shot firearms, loaded with black powder cartridges, and without a bayonet, are an inadequate weapon with which to resist the bolo rushes of an overwhelming number of fanatical outlaws. The outlaws will deliberately provoke and draw fire solely for the advantage which the cloud of smoke gives them in their bolo rushes." He recommended issue of Krag repeating carbines, arguing that even if some are lost through capture, the local bands would not be able to produce the more modern cartridges this gun required.[77] In this same report, Harry criticizes the conduct and efficiency of most municipal police agencies, within the seven provinces of his district.

In the fall, with Southern Luzon pacified, it was again time to move. On October 16, 1905, Harry was placed in Command of Central Luzon, District 1, with Headquarters in Manila. Within six months, the troops under his command had destroyed or captured most of the insurgents. These included such men as Macario Sakay, Cornelia Felizardo, Leon Villafuerte, Benito Natividad, Lucio De Vega, Francisco Carreon, and Ancieto Oruga who were the most notorious bandits found anywhere in the islands. Many of these men were subordinates of Sakay[78] and served in a variety of areas, such as Bulacan (Villafuerte), Cavite (both Felizardo and De Vega), and Batangas (Natividad and Oruga). Carreon served as second in command to Sakay, a Filipino General in the Philippine-American War. He was born during the year 1870, in Tondo, Manila. A member of the Katipunan movement of Andres Bonifacio, in 1902, he founded a Tagalog Republic in opposition to the United

---

[77] *Annual Report of the Philippine Commission, 1905, Part 3, report of the officer commanding, second district, Philippines Constabulary, Col. II. H. Bandholtz*

[78] *Macario Sacay y de León, Philipine insurgent leader and self proclaimed President*

States occupation of his country. During the early years of insurrection, he fought alongside Bonifacio in the hills of Morong Province, on the island of Luzon. On June 16, 1902, the New York Times reported that five US Cavalrymen, captured by the insurgents on May $30^{th}$, near Teresa, Morong Province, had been boloed to death by their captors.

Sakay started life with a working class background, and was apprenticed in a manufacturing shop. He also worked at various jobs, including tailor and as a barber. For a time he acted in Tagalog Dramas, where he learned of love, discipline and courage.

In 1904, Sakay and his men took the offensive and succeeded in capturing arms and ammunition on raids in Cavite and Batangas. They disguised themselves in Constabulary uniforms during these attacks, causing confusion among the American and Constabulary forces.

Administratively, Harry was appointed Acting Chief of Constabulary, in addition to being Commander of District 1, effective March 24, 1906. He established an intelligence unit, within the Constabulary. This section was responsible for gathering intelligence, mainly from local residents, regarding suspicious activity within their neighborhoods. Of particular interest were the activities of Japanese collusion with insurgent groups, political activity or plans to usurp local authority. It is reported that through these intelligence sources, Colonel Bandholtz was able to "confine the Philippine Assembly to reasonable channels." [79]

The insurgents, and his wife, however, caused not all of Harry's problems. In a letter from Colonel J. Harboard, Commander, $2^{nd}$ District, dated October 31, 1905, he is informed of a Constabulary Officer and his monetary problems.

---

[79] *Army Surveillance in America, 1775-1980, by Joan M, Jensen, Yale University Press 1991*

"The Howard case is a very nasty one. He got that negro Walker to go to Dena Maria Herrera with a hard luck story about his having lost some money belonging to a dead brother officer, "save my honor" and all that. He lied several different times about what he did with the money entrusted to him in the Manila trip including the band fund, and money held in trust for his cook; gouged Harn on a furniture trade for his commissary bill, giving away later some of the furniture that he gave to Harn to satisfy his bill; owed Walker 23 pesos, and last of all got into poor Humphrey for 250 pesos, on the plea of temporary embarrassment, new District Chief, Col Bandholtz, of course, friend of mine, if he was here would understand at once, etc. I would thank you to see this thing along and see that Humphrey gets his money!"

In a letter from the Executive Bureau, Government of the Philippines, dated November 2, 1905, Harry is notified he has been appointed Assistant Director of Constabulary. As his responsibilities increased, and his promotions awarded, he was obliged to receive guests in a formal setting, and return such favors. It was learned that May did not appreciate the social skills befitting the wife of a senior officer. Her referring to the native Filipinos in derogatory terms often embarrassed him, even made disparaging remarks about the wives of officers junior to her husband. Many times, these comments were made loud enough to insult the officers and their wives.

Also at this time, there was a lot of criticism of the Constabulary and its effectiveness was questioned in the newspapers at home. One newspaper reported, "These are harsh charges to make against the organization charged with the maintenance of public order in the Philippines. The literal truth of what has been said is easily to be established, however, if one does not assume from these general statements that the whole constabulary force and its officers are of the sort described."[80] Further into the article the author

---

[80] *October 17, 1905 Washington Evening Star*

goes on to state, "There are whole districts, notably the southern provinces of Luzon below Batangas, which is under the command of Colonel and District Commander H. H. Bandholtz, where a splendid state of order prevails, where the constabulary has been well recruited, reasonably well officered, and is held by its chief under the strictest sort of discipline, and is made to co-operate with the civil authorities and to stand in the proper relation to the Filipino officials of provinces and municipalities."

On January 22, 1906, an officer, W. A. Crossland writes to Harry, "Dear Colonel: I am broke and need to borrow $25.00 from you until payday. I have "dinero" supposed to be coming from Albay but, like pay day, it comes devilish slow." The tone of the letter suggests there existed a cordial relationship between the Harry and his subordinates. The requested money was provided and sent by messenger.

Harry amused himself with his passions for stamp collecting and horticulture. He toured the various islands looking for orchid varieties of which there were thousands. His horticultural interests may have grown beyond that of a personal interest, because in September 1909, a Memorandum issued by Headquarters, $5^{th}$ District, Philippine Constabulary, states in part: "The District Director has recently received a letter from General Bandholtz, Director of Constabulary, requesting him to try and obtain a large quantity of flowering orchids as the director is trying to secure a collection of as many varieties as possible." The memo goes on to suggest the islands where the rare varieties were to be found, gathering techniques, and shipping instructions to Headquarters. Whether these were for the personal collection of Harry, or for a Horticultural Society is not clear.

It is reported that he was a non-drinker, but had a sweet tooth. There was always a bowl of candies located on his desk. He was active in many civil or military organizations. These ran the gamut from the Masonic Lodge to Polo Clubs,

Y.M.C.A., Army and Navy Club, Spanish-American War Veterans, Horticulture Society, just to name a few. At his home in Manila, he also had a menagerie of tropical birds, monkeys, and other animals. Letters to his son often described these additions to his household animals. For exercise as well as recreation, he also took up the game of golf, playing with such notables as Generals Pershing and Leonard Wood, at various locations throughout the islands. In several letters he refers to his "plowing up the turf" at different golf courses.

On July 14, 1906, Sakay received a letter from the American Governor-General, in which he was promised amnesty for himself and his men. He turned himself in, however three days later, was arrested, tried as a bandit, convicted, and on September 13, 1907, was executed by hanging. During his trial, he and his co-defendants admitted they were guilty of the charges brought against them, but did so "from a patriotic motive in defense of the rights of their country." To counter this claim, prosecutors introduced a letter by Sakay to one of his generals, is which he states, "Direct the troops to enter the town of Teresa and carry out the following: First- Seize all such foods as pala which you can carry; also take the money, in order to defray the expenses of our soldiers and the war. Second- Arrest the Consejal, and all persons concerned with him in detaining our Commissioners, and as soon as arrested you will punish them as provided by Order 9 of April 10, 1904, prescribing that the tendon Achilles shall be cut and the fingers of both hands be crushed. Third- if the townspeople offer resistance to the troops, burn all the houses without showing mercy to the inhabitants. All the provisions of this letter have been passed by the Supreme Junta, on account of the treacherous conduct of the inhabitants of Teresa towards our commissioners."[81]

---

[81] *NY Times, Cruelty of Filipinos, Sep 29, 1907*

# Chapter Eight

# CHIEF OF CONSTABULARY

Brigadier General H. H. Bandholtz
Chief of Constabulary 1907-1913
Bandholtz Papers, UMICH

During June 1907, Harry Bandholtz was appointed Director of Constabulary, and given the rank of Brigadier General (Temporary). This placed him in command of all constabulary troops, reporting directly to the Civil Commission, which oversaw the governing of the islands comprising the Philippines. There were still insurgent uprisings in many areas, with groups stirring up disloyalty. In many eyes, the Americans merely replaced the Spaniards as occupiers and the natives resisted this occupation.

It was during this year when Harry was elected Commander of the Veteran Army of the Philippines, an organization composed of U.S. soldiers still in the islands. The following year, he was responsible for the amalgamation of this group with the United States Spanish War Veteran's, an organization in which he also held membership. This combined organization would later evolve into the Veterans of Foreign Wars.

Throughout his time with the constabulary, there were persistent rumors of Japanese intervention, and/or rumors of an actual Japanese invasion. Japanese warships were seen off the coast, apparently scouting certain areas. Often there were reports of the landing of firearms, but no large quantities of arms were ever located. Internal constabulary intelligence reports described insurgent groups meeting with Japanese Officials, raising funds for the purchase of arms.

These concerns are addressed in a July 22, 1907 letter from Harry to Captain Davis, General Staff, Ft Leavenworth, Kansas. He wrote the following as a portion: "In this connection I might add that (General) Malvar[82] recently came to my office to discuss the Japanese situation, and he told me that he realized that the Japanese would be the ruin of his country. He said he came to place himself unconditionally at my disposition and that, in case of necessity; he could turn out as many thousand loyal volunteers as the government might desire. In the beginning many of the Filipinos thought that Japanese sovereignty would be a fine thing, but they have now practically all of them changed their minds and are beginning to fall from under. The islands are swarming with Japanese, and I have located a few Japanese officers."

In a report to General Bandholtz dated August 29, 1907, Constabulary Superintendent of Information, Major R. Crane, writes: "In transmitting the copies of the enclosed papers, I have the honor to point out that since 1896, Filipino revolutionists have been intriguing with Japan and the Japanese officials with a view to bringing about the independence of the Philippines, and on account of race, color and ethnological affinities, have looked to that country

---

[82] *Miguel Malvar, (1865-1911) Filipino Revolutionary, fought against the Spanish and the Americans. Surrendering in 1902, he prospered as a farmer*

and those officials for help and sympathy in the attaining of their object.

Though since 1898-99 there is no evidence to prove that they have received any covert assistance or open countenance from Japan, there is every reason to believe that since then, and up to the present time, considerable encouragement and sympathy have been extended to these revolutionists by high Japanese officials, if not in their official capacity at least as individuals."

As history shows, the perceived threat did not materialize until some many years later. However, sporadic insurrections by small groups continued to keep the Constabulary busy.

During 1908, the entire country was relatively quiet. In a report, the Government states, "It is eminently gratifying to state that from July 1, 1908, to date (November 3, 1908), a state of complete peace has existed throughout the Archipelago--with the exception of some slight disorders caused by raids of lawless Datus and brigands in the Moro Province."

Peace overall may have been the case, but incidents continued especially in the Moro Province. One man, Captain Harold H. Elarth was in the hills of Mindanao, with a team of ten constabulary men, trying to find an insurgent group of Moros. What he encountered was a band numbering close to 1,000. He called for talks and the insurgent leader agreed. Elarth and his ten troopers, sat with the insurgent group. As the talks were going on, three of the Moros drew their weapons and attacked the constabulary men. In the ensuing battle, several Moro Tribesmen and all but three of the constabulary men were killed, when the Moros unleashed a fusillade of spears and then disappeared into the jungle. Captain Elarth, and his two surviving constabulary officers, removed the bolts from their comrades' rifles, and escaped to the safety of their barracks.[83]

---

[83] *Jungle Patrol*

The Northern Islands were considered at peace, but head hunting tribes were still active. In 1908 it was reported that 44 heads were taken in a mountainous area, Northern Luzon. There were also incidents involving the selling and use of opium, insurgent pirates attacking trading vessels, and the run of normal criminal activity to contend with.

Just two years after assuming the position of Director, Harry had to deal with a mutiny by some Constabulary Troops, in the area of Davao, on the island of Mindanao. Late evening of June 6 1909, the forty-eight men in the post were quiet in barracks, when, at a prearranged signal, twenty-three privates seized arms and broke from the barracks. Shots were fired as the escaping men were pursued through the streets. The firing was heavy, but the casualties were small. One American civilian was killed, trapped in the line of fire, and four loyal Constabulary men were wounded.[84]

Fortunately, Harry happened to be on an island hopping inspection tour at the time, and was quickly able to reinforce the company where the mutineers were assigned. As it turned out, of the men who left their barracks, 11 were captured or killed in a matter of days. The problems seem to have been caused by a lack of discipline and labor unrest caused in large part by a native officer.

On some of these inspection tours, May Bandholtz was able to accompany her husband, and they seemed to enjoy these trips together. Some stops were at mountain retreats, or the lush tropical beach areas, making these quasi business trips a most enjoyable get-a-way. During this period, his letters home were much more cheerful. He wrote to his son, Cleveland, about the various animals and birds encountered on these excursions. Their travel was by boat, frequently included visits to neighboring islands in Indonesia and Borneo. In a June 6th, 1909 letter to his assistant, Colonel J. G. Harboard, Harry relates, "Mrs. Bandholtz has developed

---

[84] *Ibid*

into almost a first-class sea traveler." It was also in 1909 that Cleveland wrote to his Dad expressing a desire to attend West Point. Dad suggested he remain at Culver Military Academy for another year, but the strong willed son took the competitive examination and was accepted. He began life as a US Military Academy Cadet in March 1910, with the Class of 1914.

In 1910, there is a new surge of reports about Japanese boats scouting remote parts of the islands, and the landing of weapons. One particular boat, named the "Otara Maru," was seen several times on different islands, taking soundings of a bay's depth, sending in small boats and occasionally bringing crates onshore. Photographers were observed taking pictures of the various locations, that were very isolated.

Because of health problems with several of his officers, Harry requested a study be made, by the Medical Department, regarding the practice of calisthenics for keeping his officers fit. In November of 1910, a report is received from Lieutenant Colonel Charles R. Woodruff, Medical Corps, U.S. Army, at Cebu. This seven-page report suggests that in tropical settings, like the Philippines, strenuous exercise may be more detrimental to the men, especially the older ones. It was suggested that a man would remain healthier if he would participate in such activities as walking, horseback riding, tennis or golf. "It has also become recently known that the production of muscles much bigger than necessary for daily life is not only useless expenditure of vital forces but a distinct disadvantage particularly for sedentary employments which to be sure require a more frail physique. A man cannot be fit at the same time to undergo great exertion and also fit to spend eight hours a day in an office chair. An officer's work is always partly sedentary, and he must then strive for a medium condition as to his muscular development."

"The following system is therefore recommended for those officers who do not take part in outdoor drills, marches and maneuvers at least three times per week: they shall at least three times a week take a ride or walk of at least a half hour at one time, or in lieu thereof indulge in an equal time in golf, tennis, bicycle riding, swimming or any other games at such times as is most pleasurable for them."

## Chapter Nine
## DIPLOMACY

The fear of Japanese interference, and intelligence reports of their scouting around the islands of the Philippines, may have caused the summoning of General Bandholtz to Japan for meetings with the Secretary of War and US Ambassador to Japan. In 1894, Japanese forces had defeated China's armies, giving them a foothold on the continent of Asia. Then in 1904-1905, the Imperial forces defeated Russian forces, strengthening their positions in Manchuria and the occupation of the Korean Peninsula. Ever since the American Punitive Expedition of 1871, diplomatic relations between America and Korea improved. In 1882, a Treaty of Amity and Commerce was signed, which included as Article 1, "There shall be perpetual peace and friendship between the President of the United States and the King of Chosen(Korea) and the citizens and subjects of their respective Governments. If other powers deal unjustly or oppressively with either Government, the other will exert their good offices, on being informed of the case, to bring about an amicable arrangement, thus showing their friendly feelings." After years of isolationist policies, Japan had been flexing her muscles and building its army and naval forces. There was concern where this would lead. Their occupation of Korea was resisted by the Korean people, but regardless of the above mentioned treaty, the United States supported a later (1911) annexation of Korea by the Japanese.

Putting on his diplomatic hat, in June 1910, Harry and May Bandholtz departed for Japan onboard the ship "Nikko Maru," for a meeting with the Secretary of War, Jacob M. Dickinson. They stopped in Hong Kong, on July $1^{st}$, where they visited with the Acting Governor, Sir Francis May.[85] Four days later, Sir Francis and his wife, Helene Barker, held a formal reception and dinner, to welcome their guests. Bidding farewell to their British hosts, the Bandholtzes set sail again on the following day, arriving in Japan on the 10$^{th}$. After a couple of train rides and another boat trip, they managed to make their way to Tokyo for meetings on the 13$^{th}$, with U.S. Ambassador Thomas J. O'Brien.

From there, they went to Yokahama where he and May met Secretary Dickinson and his party aboard the ship "Siberia." Together they all went back to Tokyo and had dinner that evening with Japan's Minister of Foreign Affairs, Count Komura.[86] This formal dinner was described as elegant and simplistic. The Count gave a speech in which he related there was a conspiracy to create misunderstanding between the United States and Japan. While stating that he felt certain the harmonious relations between the two countries had been, and were such that they could not be disturbed. Secretary Dickinson followed with an appropriate response.

In Japan at that time, the Emperor[87] was a supreme leader both religiously and politically. He was revered as a God on Earth, and lived in an isolated Imperial Palace, with his Empress and concubines. To be afforded an opportunity to see him, never mind converse with him, was a distinct honor bestowed on but a few.

Early on the 16$^{th}$, the entire party went to the Imperial Palace. The ladies were presented to the Empress while the gentlemen met the Emperor. General Bandholtz describes the protocol:

---

[85] *Sir Francis Henry May (1860 - 1922) was a British colonial administrator who became Governor of Hong Kong.*
[86] *Marquis Komura Jutarō (26 October 1855 – 26 November 1911) was a statesman and diplomat in Meiji period Japan.*
[87] *The Meiji Emperor (November 3, 1852 — July 30, 1912) was the 122nd emperor of Japan according to the traditional order of succession, reigning from February 3, 1867 until his death.*

"In approaching His Imperial Majesty you remained at the threshold to make a profound bow, advance halfway across the room, repeat the bow and advance towards His Majesty and make a third bow directly in front of him after which he will recognize this, extending his hand which you are supposed to fondly grasp, drop and wait a second to see if His Majesty begins to address you. In my case he asked if I were the officer that was stationed in the Philippines. I replied that I was. He then asked me how long I had been there, to which I replied nearly ten years. He stated that 10 years was a very long time. I agreed with him, and we separated. The gentlemen were then marched over to meet the Empress, at which a like ceremony was repeated." Whether the Emperor spoke English, or whether they talked through an interpreter is a matter of conjecture. Harry's diary suggests they were able to communicate on a personal basis.

He goes on to describe being ushered into a magnificent banqueting hall where members of the Royal Family, several high officers of the Government, the Army and the Navy were present. The luncheon was comparable to the dinner of the Foreign Minister, elegant but simple. The courses were just the right number and just the right length. Many of the knives, forks and spoons were solid gold. When the luncheon ended, Their Imperial Majesties departed and the rest of our party was shown through the Imperial Palace. That evening, Ambassador O'Brien gave a dinner quite as elaborate.

The next day, the entire American Party shared a luncheon at the Arsenal Gardens, hosted by the Japanese Army Chief of Staff. Thirty-seven General Officers, from both the Imperial Army and Navy, were in attendance. From this affair, they traveled by train to Kobe, where they boarded the "Siberia," and headed back to the Philippines, arriving, on July 24th.

President Taft wired the Emperor of Japan thanking him for the cordial welcome received by Secretary Dickinson and his party,

*"Beverly, Mass July 17, 1910*

*The Emperor of Japan, Tokyo*

*I wish to express to your majesty my deep appreciation of the generous and courteous hospitality extended to Secretary Dickinson and his party during their visit to Japan. The expression of cordial welcome evoked strengthens the bond of friendship between the two countries.*

*William H. Taft"*


The emperor responded with a telegram of his own, in which he states,

*"I thank you for your kind telegram. It has been my great pleasure that I had the opportunity of seeing Secretary Dickinson."*

In 1910, the Philippine Commission, by unanimous proclamation, requested that General Bandholtz's current appointment be made permanent, making him a Brigadier General in the regular Army. Unfortunately, this resolution was not acted upon by the powers in Washington.

## Chapter Ten

## MINING INVESTMENTS

During his time in the Philippines, Harry and others invested in land claims for mining operations. Lieutenant George M. Wray, of the Philippine Scouts, first discovered coal on the island of Polillo, in 1904. Early analyses showed the coal to be of good quality and abundant. Wray, with Harry, and two other investors, formed the Polillo Land Company, to lease lands containing the coal deposits. The company planned to develop the mining operations, and would then sell the coal for steam-powered ships. Government contracts were a distinct possibility since the US Navy was purchasing its coal from Japan. While it may have produced some profits, there were many obstacles and headaches. This was another area where May Bandholtz criticized her husband's business dealings, telling him he had absolutely no business sense

Polillo Island is a kidney-shaped island located 25 km off the eastern coast of Luzon mainland and due east of Manila. It is 50-km long and about 11 to 28-km wide. The island could be reached only by boat to the Municipality of Burdeous. As the costs of geological analyses and land surveys grew, the company took on additional shareholders. The Navy needed cheaper coal for its ships, and the search went on. Coal was located on several of the islands, and it depended upon where it would be obtained most economically.

Lieutenant H. L. Wigmore, US Army Corps of Engineers, was dispatched to the islands of Bataan and Polillo, during 1904, to evaluate the coal found at both places. His report, dated July 11, 1905,[88] summarizes that coal, much better than the currently purchased Japanese coal, had been located

---

[88] *Report on Examination of the Coal Deposits on Polillo Island," Annual Reports of the War Department, Volume XIII, Part 4, US Government Printing Office 1905*

on both islands, in great quantities. However, access to the coal, and the islands themselves, made it much more feasible and less expensive to develop mining operations on the Island of Bataan. Still, the investors held on to their dreams of wealth.

In a March 1, 1910 letter to former Chief of Constabulary, Brigadier General Allen, Harry writes: "Herewith I am enclosing a memorandum of the agreement entered into in regard to the coal proposition. The Governor General thinks it is the best we could expect under the circumstances, and I for one am getting tired of having it drag out indefinitely. As our claims expire in April, will you please send me your check for $150 for the expense of re-staking and clearing out? Wray will have to take a leave of absence to get the whole thing in shape."

In July of that same year, Bandholtz wrote to some of the shareholders, "It is with regret that I beg to inform you that the negotiations between Polillo Land Company and Swift and Company for the disposition of the coal lands fell through, due mainly to unfortunate circumstances, when the coal expert was brought over to the Philippines for the express purpose of inspecting the Cebu, Bataan, and Polillo deposits.

Before he had finished with Cebu, he fell seriously ill and was obliged to return to the States."

It must have been the chance of recouping lost money, and hopes for large gains, that kept the interest in the operation going for at least another three years. Maybe Mrs. Bandholtz was right when she stated that her husband had "no business sense." How much Harry profited or lost has not been determined.

Coal was not the only commodity the officers were investing in. However, the practice was stopped during late 1913 or early 1914, the Governor-General[89] decreed that the officers sell all of their stock in Filipino Companies. Governor Harrison set about with a Filipinization Program, replacing Americans with Filipinos in the Legislature and Civil Service. Critics of the policy resented his efforts, including those military officers who had been investing in coal, lumber and other interests.

Harry wrote to Colonel Harboard, on January 21, 1914, "You have, of course, heard about the satisfactory sale of the stock in the Kolambugan Lumber Co. and presumably, ere this, have received your cash for your holdings at par. I am glad that you came out so well. The action of the Governor-General in forcing us all to sell is a disappointment to me, for I would like to have held onto my stock. I believe it is going to pay far more than we could get for any equal investment in the United States.

Your profit is especially gratifying to me, as I believe you once told me that you made your purchase because you had faith in my business judgment."

The Kolambungan Lumber Company had been established in June 1912, and put many people to work. Although the company name has changed many times, lumber is still a large part of the industry in the Kolambungan area of Lanao Province.

---

[89] *Francis Burton Harrison was Governor-General from Oct 6, 1913 until March 5, 1921, appointed by President Woodrow Wilson*

## Chapter Eleven
## THE MOROS

After the pleasant interlude, visiting Hong Kong and Japan, it takes just a few days to get back into the business of running the Constabulary. At this time, General John J. Pershing was Military Governor of Moro Province, still being plagued with frequent uprisings by tribal leaders. He had been visiting with General Bandholtz and requesting more help from the Constabulary. On July 17$^{th}$ 1910 he writes:

*"Dear General Bandholtz: I have received a copy of a letter written to you by Mr. Crowhurst, and am very glad to hear this additional testimony from Crowhurst that Gilshauser[90] is doing so well in Davao. The Davao situation is going to be solved by such men as Gilshauser, and we have a number of them in the Gulf. I believe that all of the officers stationed there are doing their best to make that experiment a success. I have spent considerable time with them, and intend to keep constantly in touch with the situation. With very best regards to Mrs. Bandholtz and yourself, in which Mrs. Pershing joins, I remain, as always,*

*Yours sincerely, John J. Pershing."*

The reader may recall from the brief descriptions of battles with the Moro Tribesman, they were fanatical warriors, with no fear of death. The Sulu Moro had evolved the rite of running "juramentado" as a means of combat. This meant he would become a rabid, wild-running individual, who, with his unsheathed barong or kris, waged a personal Holy War. Binding his body in certain ways, he could continue to fight even with what many would consider fatal wounds. The

---

[90] *Henry Gilsheuser, (1881-) Germen Emigrant, US Army Officer assigned to Philippine Constabulary*

Moro seemed impervious to pistol and rifle fire, and the shotgun became a weapon of choice for the Constabulary Officer. This fanaticism is also the reason why the US Military abandoned the .38 Caliber revolver, as a sidearm, and adopted the .45 Caliber Colt Model 1911 Pistol as a more effective handgun.

According to the Moro belief, it was possible for a man, and his kris, to be transformed from the miserable nipa shacks of the Sulu shores to the scented gardens of Paradise where the houris (nymphs) waited. "Therein shall be the damsels with retiring glances whom no man hath touched before them. Theirs shall be the houris, with large, dark eyes, like pearls hidden in their shells, in recompense of their labors past."[91]

It had also been learned that the Moro could be an amphibian. If he were beaten in a jungle fight he would take to sea, out of range of Constabulary activities. To combat this, a naval task force of four small gunboats worked in conjunction with the Constabulary sinking the Moro boats while they were at sea.

The Moro situation was causing discord within the Constabulary and with Governor Pershing. On the one hand, the Insular Government was reducing the size of the Constabulary for financial reasons, but Pershing wanted more assistance from them in handling the insurrectionists. He felt that his province was being short-changed by the central government of the Philippines. Harry, always the diplomat, writes to both General Pershing and his District Commander of Constabulary of Mindanao, Colonel Mark Hersey, urging their cooperation with one another to accomplish the missions of both offices.

During this same period, there was talk of consolidating the Constabulary with the Philippine Scouts, a truly military organization. General Bandholtz thought such a merger would give him additional manpower, and yet save the US

---

[91] *Jungle Patrol*

Government substantially through the elimination of the Scout hierarchy. Others, however, did not want to see the two units merge. There was also a movement afoot to get the Philippine Government to do away with the Constabulary altogether.

A memorandum from Major Crane, of the Information Division, dated August 25 1910, suggests that this movement to dissolve the Constabulary is based in large part on the capture of one Felipe Salvador, who was believed by some to be "beyond the reach" of the Constabulary. He had thousands of followers, in many provinces, was well protected, and had several friends in politics, both local and national. Neither the amalgamation of the Constabulary-Scouts, or the dissolution of the Constabulary took place, so it remained business as usual.

During February of 1911, Harry and May returned to the United States on a leave of absence. This was their first trip back since 1904. Before leaving, however, he wrote a letter to Manuel L. Quezon, a long time friend and Resident Commissioner of the Philippines, in Washington, D.C. In the letter, Harry advised Mr. Quezon about the inflammatory articles in the Philippine Press, and the actions within the legislature causing a widening of the gap of understanding between the US and the Philippines. Quezon was a proponent for Philippine Independence, but felt it would only be accomplished by cooperation with the United States. In another letter, dated January 9, 1911, he advises a subordinate, Lieutenant Colonel John R. White, that he would look into his citizenship case, with the words "*It is a most rotten condition of affairs that subjects men like you to the humiliation, expense and worry you are now undergoing when it is so easy for others who really render the government no services whatever to obtain their papers.*"

For the trip, they were to take the ship, "Manchuria," on February 10th, from Manila to San Francisco, spend a couple of days there and then continue on to Constantine. He also planned on a stopover in Chicago on the way to West Point in June. They visited son, Cleveland, at West Point, where the General attended "June Week Activities," and a reunion of the Association of Graduates.

Upon their return to Manila, getting back into his duties, he planned a business journey to Java, in the Dutch East Indies, to observe and evaluate the policing polices of the Dutch, as regards the native population of Indonesia. They had been controlling the islands for three centuries and had learned a lot during that time frame. It was in March of 1911 when Harry and May sailed to Java, where they toured the Dutch colonies for a couple of weeks.

Harry received a letter, dated July 12, 1911, from General John J. Pershing, in reference to the discord between himself and Constabulary Colonel Hershey, mentioned above. He assures the Director that "I have gone over the whole subject of orders with Colonel Hershey and there is no sort of doubt or difference as to the view we both take of what should be done."

Pershing goes on to state that regular troops are preferred when dealing with organized insurrection, however feels the Constabulary is necessary, and valuable when chasing down murderers or other criminals. He fully intends to use regular Army troops, Constabulary and Scouts to their greatest advantage, to pacify his province. He mentions that Davao is now clear of organized insurgent groups, but he must deal with thieves and assassins. However, in Lanao there are still outlaws at large which "I am determined to capture or exterminate."

In August of 1911, the Governor General of the Philippines, William Cameron Forbes, scheduled a tour of the major cities and towns of the southern provinces by motor launch, taking with him commissioners and bureau chiefs. This so-called "floating government," was to be preceded by General Bandholtz, onboard the Constabulary Launch "Polillo." He was to schedule "town meetings," and ensure that the

Governor General had a "full house" wherever he stopped to speak. In a letter written by General Bandholtz, dated September 13, 1911, he describes his views, "I suppose it is needless to tell you that although there was a fair amount of superficial enthusiasm at the various places visited, yet arriving as I did at places like Cebu and Iloilo in advance of the distinguished party, it was evident that any enthusiasm shown was a very thin veneer. In Cebu, in particular, there was considerable grumbling. A number of the party themselves were a pretty dilapidated outfit by the time they got as far as Iloilo and their enthusiasm needed to be encouraged, in many cases, by copious draughts of Scotch and soda."

On September $3^{rd}$, 1911, Harry wrote to President William H. Taft, advising him on occurrences in the Philippines. Taft had been Governor General of the Islands earlier. In particular, he addressed their mutual friend, Manuel Quezon, and how well liked he was by the Filipinos, and their intention to have him as a member of the Assembly. However, Quezon was also very valuable in his position in Washington.

Lieutenant Colonel John R. White, one of his subordinates, was going to the Washington area, on leave. Colonel White was a Canadian by birth, and had been trying to obtain US citizenship. On October 13, 1911, General Bandholtz wrote the following letter:

*"To Whom it may concern:*

*The bearer of this, Lieutenant Colonel John Roberts White, Philippine Constabulary, has served continuously with the United States Army and Philippine Constabulary since April 20, 1899. Through no fault of his own, and owing to the peculiar status of the Philippine Islands as United States Territory, he has been unable to secure his final papers as an American citizen to which he is entitled. I consider Colonel White to possess the highest qualifications for citizenship. His faithful and gallant services under the*

*American flag have signalized him in the Constabulary and I request that all consideration be shown by those who can help him to become an American citizen.*

Brigadier General, U.S.A.,
Chief, Philippine Constabulary"

The situation within Moro Province was not improving so General Pershing ordered the disarming of the Moros. This was bound to cause problems with the native population. The Constabulary was under orders to take every barong, campilane or kris they encountered in the course of a patrol. It was desperate, bloody work. The Moro lived with arms for centuries, in a land where the sign of manhood was his ability to use his bladed weapons.

One constabulary lieutenant is quoted as stating, "It was a terrible thing to take the barong away from a Joloano Moro. You were taking away his visible masculine characteristic. You made him a woman and less than a woman. Most any Constabulary officer could kill a Moro and take his blade. Some officers did. It was all a part of the day's work to them. When they met a Moro wearing a barong they called for the blade. If he resisted or started to run, they shot him and entered it in their report. But to take a weapon from a Moro required skill and patience, and I could not find it in me to kill them in cold blood because they stood on their tribal rights."[92] In many cases, diplomacy worked much better that the threat of disarming, however, the Moros were not pacified until well into 1913.

When the Moros, mostly, if not all Muslims, fought a defensive battle, all involved, men, women and children, would retreat to a high ground, where they would fight to the last. This occurred at Bud Bagsak, in Sulu, during June of 1912, and signaled the end of the Moro-American War.[93]

---

[92] *Jungle Patrol*
[93] *Keeping the Spirit of 1896 Alive*, by Onofre D. Corpuz, Ph.D., U. of Philippines

All welcomed pacification of this important tribe. They had been a fierce opponent and fought bravely in every instance. The government now would endeavor to get the Moros more involved with the government in constructive ways.

## Chapter Twelve

## PACIFICATION

In a letter to President Taft, dated October 30, 1911, General Bandholtz relates that the disarming of the Moros is progressing but that it is a troublesome venture. He also notified the President of the killing, by the Contabulary, of Otoy, a famous insurgent leader.

The killing of Otoy by the constabulary in 1911 marked the passing of the last of a series of mountain chiefs who had exercised a very powerful influence over the hill people and had claimed for themselves supernatural powers. With the death of Otoy, General Bandholtz states in another letter, the Constabulary will now be able to use "prevention rather than curative measure in dealing with the natives."

Earlier in October, he received notification from the Philippine Exposition that he has been appointed to a Committee on Horticulture, and that his presence was required at certain meetings. At about the same time, word is received from Colonel Hershey that the program to disarm the Moros has caused problems of desertion within his companies. He requested that three addition companies of Constabulary, from Manila be dispatched to replace his troops. This caused a reaction from General Bandholtz, "you can imagine what a fine kettle of fish we would have if we introduced three Moro companies into Manila and sent three Christian companies to Mindanao!" His instructions were to get rid of those constabulary troops who were causing unrest and augment his existing companies with new recruits from throughout the islands.

Also during 1911, a rash of home burglaries were brought to the attention of the Constabulary, within the immediate Manila area. The victims were prominent or wealthy persons. Many burglaries were included in this same report, nineteen in all, each having the same basic modus operandi; that being night-time entry, occupants sleeping within the house, and only currency and small pieces of jewelry taken. These stolen items are easily disposed of and left little chance of being recovered. Occurring while the occupants were present made them feel all the more violated, and they were demanding action from the Governor General.

As the year 1911, comes to a close, General Bandholtz is planning another trip home. His proposed trip would take him from Manila, again aboard the ship "Manchuria," to San Francisco. Originally he had hoped to travel through the Suez Canal to Europe and then on to New York, where he could see his son at West Point. What caused the change of routing is not quite clear, but in a letter dated December 23, 1911, he outlines his plans to a Judge in the Philippines. He writes, "In strict confidence I may tell you that my departure has been rather hastened by the fact that there is a possibility that General Edwards will be transferred to the line about May 1$^{st}$ and my friends thought it would be advisable to be in the States prior to that time. I don't know as it will do a particle of good, but it can do no harm and will only slightly change our plans, and we can arrange to return through Europe."

Certain members of Congress were pushing to have General Bandholtz promoted to Brigadier General in the Regular Army, and thought it better if he were in the United States to do some politicking on his own. The Governor General of the Philippines had forwarded letters with this same recommendation. Add to this the fact that General Bandholtz's mother had fallen ill, and was urging her son to come home as quickly as possible. Regardless, the plans were altered and General Bandholtz writes to an Army Captain in San Francisco, "I want to take a train for Chicago the second day after our arrival (in San Francisco). What I want, however, is to engage a stateroom, a compartment or an apartment ---or whatever they call the damn things---in a sleeper for Chicago. If you can, without serious inconvenience to yourself, make tentative arrangements along these lines, we shall be deeply grateful." His plans included a visit to May's home in Chicago, his own home, in Constantine, and a trip to West Point for Cleveland's graduation from the Military Academy in June.

Harry and May did make the trip home. They sailed on the S.S. Manchuria, from Hong Kong, on February 10, 1912, arriving in San Francisco on March 8$^{th}$. According to the ship's manifest, this time they carried seventeen pieces of luggage between them, which included many souvenirs. They were able to attend son Cleveland's graduation, and brought him back home. While at West Point, Harry was able to again attend the meetings of the Association of Graduates. No action was taken, however, on the bid for a Brigadier's appointment.

Returning to Manila, Harry is brought up to date on occurrences during his absence. He also reviewed intelligence reports from the chief of that section of the Constabulary. In early 1913, Harry was able to organize and direct an operation to capture complete and up to date plans of the American defenses on the island of Corregidor. Maps of areas surrounding Manila accompanied these plans, which showed the location of artillery, including their fields of fire, protecting the approaches to Manila. The plans had been stolen by an employee, turned over to insurgents, who planned on getting them to the Japanese, through Artemio Ricarte, who was now living in Japan. This was a spectacular intelligence coup and once again the Bureau of Insular Affairs recommended Harry be given a permanent general's star. President Wilson had also verbally promised Harry that he would be appointed Chief of Insular Affairs, but Harry soon was ordered back home. Instead of a promotion to flag rank, he was instead reverted back to his permanent rank as Major.

*Special Orders*            *War Department*
*No. 165*            *Washington, July 17$^{th}$, 1913*

18. By direction of the President, Maj. Harry H. Bandholtz, Infantry, is relieved from duty as chief of the Philippine Constabulary, to take effect September 1, 1913, and will proceed by the first available transport to San Francisco, Cal., and upon arrival report by telegraph to the Adjutant General of the Army for further orders. By orders of the Secretary of War:

W. W. Wotherspoon.

The Idaho Daily Statesman recorded that: "*Army Man Loses Rank—Former Head of Philippines Constabulary Returns to Become Major—Harry Hill Bandholtz, U.S.A., returned to the United States from the Philippines to become major, instead of a brigadier general, a rank which he has held as head of the Philippines constabulary. His return to his regular army rank is necessitated by a recent order of the war department limiting the period of an officer's detachment to three years. General Bandholtz went to the Philippines in 1900 as a captain in the Second Infantry. During his service he received from the natives the unique honor for an American soldier of being elected governor of one of the provinces.*"[94]

We can only speculate what happened during that last year in the Philippines. Harry was considered by many to be one of the very best leaders in the American Army. He was well liked and respected by his fellow officers, and by those under his command. He was constantly being recommended for advancement to general, on a permanent basis. Politics played a part, but so did the outspoken May Bandholtz. Harry did not get the assignment promised by President Wilson, nor the promotion to Brigadier General.

---

[94] *America's Genealogy Bank, online*

Harry was a close friend with General Leonard Wood, who frequently criticized President Wilson's policies. Wood and Harry were also supporters of Theodore Roosevelt, another critic of Wilson. Wilson would later relieve Wood as Chief of Staff of the Army, replacing him with John J, Pershing. Harry and Pershing also got on well, having served together on previous occasions, both in Mexico and Cuba. Even with Pershing's support, the much-deserved promotion to Brigadier General did not materialize.[95]

The situation with May was a different story. She was a constant complainer, and very critical of her husband, privately and publicly. He was frequently accused of infidelity, a charge he vehemently denied. She criticized Harry for a variety of things and embarrassed him in front of his fellow officers and government officials, by using disparaging remarks towards other officer's wives, and the native Filipinos. Many of these remarks were very hurtful to the subjects of those comments. During this time there were indications of the mental illness that would eventually cause her to be institutionalized.

---

[95] *Biography of MG Harry Hill Bandholtz 1864-1925*

## Chapter Thirteen

## BACK TO ARMY SERVICE

In September 1913, upon completion of his duties in the Philippines, Major Bandholtz was assigned to the 29$^{th}$ Infantry, and commander of Fort Porter, New York. The original military reservation was purchased by the Federal Government on December 30, 1814 and consisted of only 200 acres. Named in honor of General Peter Buell Porter, famous for his service during the War of 1812, the post was constructed from 1838 until the mid-1840s when a fort rose on the high ground near the shore overlooking the juncture of Lake Erie and the Niagara River, near Buffalo. The post remained in service until the 1920s, when the land was sold for construction of the Peace Bridge between the US and Canada. Harry remained at Fort Porter for all of 1914, but during March of 1915 was transferred to the 30th Infantry at Plattsburg Barracks, N.Y. and promoted to the rank of Lieutenant Colonel.

Plattsburg Barracks is located on the west bank of Lake Champlain, in upper New York State, near the Canadian Border. It is the site of two great, closely related events in American History. During the War of 1812, on September 11, 1814, a British Army of 14,000 marched down from Canada, and encountered a much smaller American Force, mostly militia, near Plattsburg. The strong force of British regulars, who had been pushing their way south and east with such determination, seemed to falter. No one seemed to notice a lone horseman entering the American lines. Word arrived from the forts that Lieutenant Thomas MacDonough had prevailed in the Bay. As the welcome news spread through the ranks, loud cheers were heard. Unnerved, the British fell back, beginning a retreat to the safety of the occupied village.

On nearby Lake Champlain, a severe naval battle had taken place, between British and American ships. The American Commander, MacDonough won the day, destroying the British fleet. The surviving British officers boarded Mac Donough's flagship, Saratoga, to offer their swords (in surrender). When he saw the officers, MacDonough replied, "Gentlemen, return your swords to your scabbards, you are worthy of them"[96].

Following the War of 1812, 40 log barracks were built within the pentagon complex formed by Forts Brown, Moreau, Gaines, Tompkins, and Scott. In 1838, three stone barracks were constructed on a military post south of this complex, and the name changed to Plattsburg Barracks. The Army maintained a presence at Plattsburg until 1944.

As Harry settled in at Plattsburg, a Serbian assassinated the Archduke Ferdinand, heir to the throne of Austria-Hungary, in Sarajevo, Bosnia. A retaliatory raid against Serbia led to the forming of alliances, and ultimately to the World War. Germany and Austria-Hungary joined to become the Central Powers, while France, Great Britain, and Russia became the Entente. Other countries soon followed, Turkey joining with the Central Powers, followed by Bulgaria. Italy joined the Entente in 1915.

Feelings in the United States were that they should remain neutral, as it was a European problem, and should be settled by Europeans. However, it was not long before British and French Troops were in desperate straits. War raged from the lowlands of France, to the mountains of Northern Italy, and Bulgaria. Romania had sided with the Entente, but with the Turkish closing of the Dardanelles, relief supplies could not get through to the Black Sea, and Romania's ports. She was totally dependent on Russia for arms and ammunition.

In May of 1916, a German submarine, off the southern coast of Ireland, sank the Lusitania, a British Ocean Liner,

---

[96] *War of 1812 Webpage, http://war1812.tripod.com/batplatts.html*

carrying a large number of American passengers. One hundred twenty eight Americans, out of a total of one hundred thirty nine, lost their lives. Included in these numbers were several well known, and wealthy personages, including the writer Elbert Hubbard, author of "A Message to Garcia," and his wife.

On May 1st, the Lusitania, had departed from New York City, amid warnings from the German Embassy, that all British Ships, sailing to, or near, the British Isles were subject to the rules of war and could be destroyed. The circumstances surrounding the sinking were blurred by accusations and counter charges. Germany was convinced the Lusitania was carrying munitions, contrary to maritime regulations, while Britain claimed she was an unarmed passenger liner. In any case, British Naval Warships, which were to escort the ship through the English Channel, left their positions going to anchorage in Queenstown, Ireland, knowing full well that German submarines were active in her line of travel. Other sources speculate Britain was so anxious to get America into the war, that she sacrificed her own ship, knowing it would rile the population of the United States. Regardless of the cause, the sinking did arouse Americans who began to chant for revenge.

America had other things to worry about. On its southern border, Mexican bandits had been striking into the United States, since 1913. On March 9, 1916, Francisco "Pancho" Villa's forces attacked the town of Columbus, New Mexico, in retaliation for an arms deal[97] that had gone sour. The Mexican troops did not do well, and were routed by American defenders, but only after they laid waste to the town. As a result of this raid, the Americans issued a call to arms, and a well-equipped army went into Chihuahua, Mexico. While Villa managed to elude capture, the Americans took this opportunity to test all of their

---

[97] *An American dealer had allegedly sold them movie blanks in place of real ammunition, http://www.ojinaga.com/villa/index.html*

modernized military equipment, in anticipation of their entry in the World War. The expedition ended and all efforts to capture Villa were unsuccessful.

After one year, at Plattsburg, Colonel Bandholtz was again on the move. On May 12, 1916, he traveled with his unit to Fort Sam Houston, Texas, and on June 23, was ordered on to Eagle Pass.

A month later, the New York State National Guard Division had been mobilized and moved to the Mexican border to participate in Brigadier General John Pershing's sortie into Mexico. On July 16$^{th}$, Harry was appointed Chief of Staff of the New York Division. Under the supervision of General John F. O'Ryan, Harry completely reorganized the command, in an up-to-date and efficient manner. The National Guard troops were not used for the punitive expedition and soon returned home.

Col H. Bandholtz. With permission
Military Police Museum

Upon return of the Division to New York, Harry was appointed as Senior Inspector/Instructor of the New York National Guard, but when the New York Division was being reorganized into the 27$^{th}$ Infantry Division, he was again appointed Chief of Staff. He was responsible for all details of the reorganization and subsequent training at Spartanburg, SC. The re-designation took place on July 20, 1917.

In Europe, the war was still raging, and pleas were coming in from France and England for assistance. The United States had been providing munitions, but was not yet eager to commit troops. Germans, at the time, were the largest ethnic group in America, and there was sympathy for that nation. Others considered England as the "Mother Country," and France was a major ally during our fight for independence. Neutrality still seemed the best option. However, America had military observers in Europe learning the lessons of warfare.

Relations between the United States and Germany had deteriorated. The Kaiser had stopped the sinking of passenger liners, after Lusitania, but continued operations against all other shipping. Two explosions, in ammunition storage areas, in New Jersey, during 1916 and early 1917, were blamed on German Agents. Shortly thereafter, on April 6, Congress declared war on Germany. In June, the first units of Pershings Army were landing in France. He himself, accompanied a part of the 16$^{th}$ Infantry Regiment, the first among many who would eventually serve in Europe.

Once again, the United States was totally unprepared for war. American inventors Hiram Maxim, John Browning and Isaac Newton Lewis, had developed automatic machineguns which were wreaking havoc throughout the world. They had been offered to US Army Ordnance years earlier, and each was rejected as being too wasteful of ammunition. Therefore, the Army of the United States was still using antiquated weapons. She had adopted a new, first rate battle rifle calling it the United States Rifle, Caliber .30, Model 1903. This Mauser influenced design, was developed at Springfield Arsenal, and used a new cartridge, far more efficient than that of the Krag Rifle. Frequent design changes slowed production but over 800,000 rifles were produced at two arsenals, before US entry into World War I. These numbers were not nearly sufficient for arming the huge army, which would be sent to Europe. Firearms manufacturers were geared up for production of British Rifles, so they were required to alter these designs to accept the new US cartridge. These rifles were issued to supplement the Springfield, and became known as the Model 1917 Enfield. The US had a total of 1,100 machineguns, of various makes and models, barely enough to have four guns per regiment.[98] The first units arriving in France were issued the Chatchat French Machinegun, an ugly and cumbersome gun, prone to breakage and stoppages. Many were tossed aside as scrap, by the US troops. Fortunately, John M. Browning, had developed a series of automatic weapons, which would soon be in mass production. A pistol of his design had been in service since 1911, as the US semiautomatic pistol, caliber .45.

With war preparations under way, the chances were good that Harry would be moved overseas. He was in the process of reorganizing and training a division for combat. May Bandholtz passed along rumors that Harry wanted to remain at home, even telling some of his military associates that he was unwilling to serve. Nothing could have been further from the truth.

During August to November 1917, Harry did go to Europe, where he served as an observer, first with the British, and then with the French. He was with the British at Langemarck, Belgium, located about 4 miles northeast of Ypres. The Battle of Langemarck, one of the fiercest battles of the war, began with a tremendous artillery barrage. Not only were the many German strong points bombarded, but also a creeping artillery barrage was laid down to cover the British infantry advance. A German counter-barrage fell behind the British front line and a furious storm of machine-

---

[98] *The World's Machine Guns in the Great War*, by P. V. Garland, Emma Gee

gun and sniper fire met them shortly after the attack began. The battle ended on August 25$^{th}$, with a British victory.

In France, the Chemin Des Dames lay in part of the Western Front held by French armies. It was the scene of several bloody battles during the war. The strategic ridge stood between the Germans and Paris. It was in this area where Harry served with French forces. On 23 October, after the French victory in the Malmaison battle, German forces retreated to north of the Ailette valley.

After serving as an observer, Colonel Bandholtz returned to the United States. He sailed from Bordeaux, on the S.S. Rochambeau, arriving in New York in November. In the following month he was promoted to Brigadier General, in the Regular Army. Two months later he was given command of the 58$^{th}$ Brigade, of the 29$^{th}$ Infantry Division, which was commanded by Major General Charles G. Morton. Harry had served with Morton earlier in his career. He joined the unit at Camp McClellan, Alabama.

Prior to his return to France, with his brigade, problems worsened between Harry and May, and they were legally separated. At this time she again seemed to experience periods of delusion. The press reported that May Bandholtz had become insane after fearing her husband had been lost at sea, when a ship he was on had been torpedoed by the Germans. It was not until he returned to the United States that he was able to contradict the erroneous reports which had been published. The ship sunk was indeed one he had sailed on, but the sinking was a year after his voyage!

The 58$^{th}$ Infantry Brigade was composed of the 115$^{th}$ and 116$^{th}$ Infantry Regiments, each with 3700 soldiers, 112th Machinegun Battalion, of 800 men with 260 machineguns, along with support units. During May the 29$^{th}$ Infantry Division was ordered to France. The 58$^{th}$ Brigade was transported from Camp McClellan by Southern Railway, to Hoboken, New Jersey, a portion of the greater New York Harbor. Other units departed from Newport News, Virginia, where they met their ships. Harry led this brigade to France on June 15, sailing from New York on the transport Covington. Other elements of his brigade were transported on the ships George Washington and the Dante Alighieri. Loading of the ships was done with a great deal of attention to security. Formed into a single line, each man was identified by name and number before being allowed to board his ship.

The convoy left New York, under Navy escort, camouflaged transports, being escorted by cruisers and destroyers, led by the battleship Texas, to guard against the German submarines which were patrolling the Atlantic. Abandon boat drills were a daily activity during the crossing. After several days, the convoy arrived safely in French waters without any submarine encounters, although there had been alerts and gunfire at false sightings. Off the coast, the convoy separated and the ships carrying the $58^{th}$ Infantry Brigade landed at Brest, France, except for the Dante Alihieri which went into Bordeaux.

The men had been in France just briefly when the division was ordered to a training center at Prouthy. The rapid advance of the German Army towards Paris required that every available unit be moved towards the front. Early morning of July $1^{st}$, saw the division moved by train for Champlitte, Haute Saone. The division post office was established on July $4^{th}$, at Prouthy, Division Headquarters, and mail delivery was begun, using a Frenchman's wheelbarrow.

On July $16^{th}$, the division was again on the move, by train, this time being added to a "quiet" portion of the front lines. Division Headquarters, Prouthy, was closed and re-established near the city of Belfort. After some final training, the $29^{th}$ Division replaced the $32^{nd}$ US Division at the front.

The $58^{th}$ Infantry Brigade was responsible for holding the Gildwiller-Balschwiller area of the front lines, in a sector called "Rougemont." It was recorded, "the woods were infested with snipers who although silent during the day were very active at night." Fortunately, no one was hit during this period. On the 31$^{st}$ of July, however, a German raid on an outpost of the 115$^{th}$ Infantry, 58$^{th}$ Brigade, resulted in the death of a few men while several others were wounded, before the Germans were repelled.

From that point forward, the size and intensity of attacks increased. Bandholtz had command of his brigade until just prior to the division leaving the Alsace Sector. While commander of the 58$^{th}$ Infantry he participated in the Somme Offensive: Oise-Aisne, Ypres-Eys; and Meuse-Argonne: Center Sector, Haute Alsace.[99]

On September 25$^{th}$ General Bandholtz was pulled from the line, reassigned to A.E.F. Headquarters, in Chaumont, and appointed Provost Marshal General.[100]

---

[99] *Obit, USMA Association of Graduates, Superintendant's Report 1927*
[100] *History of the Twenty-ninth Division, by John A. Cutchins,* <u>Press of MacCalla & Co</u>, *Philadelphia 1921*

## Chapter Fourteen

# ORGANIZING THE MILITARY POLICE

Prior to World War I (except in time of war) there was no provision for the position of Provost Marshal General (PMG), never mind a Provost Marshal General's Department. There were soldiers who performed military police duties, but these were regular troops assigned a temporary duty, generally at the division level.

On April 16, 1917, Congress declared a state of war existed between the United States and the Imperial German Government. This meant a great increase in the size of the US Armed Forces, and the transport of a huge army to the European theater of operations. More than 2 million US troops eventually reached Europe but a large number arrived too late to see any action. Major General Enoch Crowder was appointed Provost Marshal General of the Army, but he also served as Judge Advocate General. His main function was enforcement of the Selective Service laws.

In the May 24, 1918 edition of The Washington Post, there appeared an article entitled, "Text of Amendment to Draft Regulations Announced by Provost Marshal General." Basically the amendment addressed the question of compelling men not engaged in a useful occupation to immediately get themselves employed in a useful venture or face conscription. Major General Crowder is quoted as saying, "This regulation provides that after July 1 any registrant who is found by a local board to be a habitual idler, or not engaged in some useful occupation, shall be summoned before the board, given a chance to explain, and in the absence of a satisfactory explanation to be inducted into the military service of the United States." This regulation also applied to men engaged in food service in public areas, elevator operators, doormen, attendants at sporting venues, theaters, those in domestic service, and sales clerks in local stores. Persons in these occupations would not be allowed to claim deferment. It further states that no ruling had been made regarding men involved with sport. "No ruling as to whether baseball players or persons engaged in golf, tennis, or any other sport came under the regulations regarding idlers or nonessential pursuits will be made until a specific case has been appealed to the provost marshal general's office."

General John J. Pershing, in forming the American Expeditionary Force (A.E.F), appointed Lieutenant Colonel Hanson E. Ely, an infantry officer, as the first Provost Marshal General. After only one month, Lieutenant Colonel William H. Allaire replaced Ely. Lieutenant Colonel John C. Groome, in turn, assumed the position after one year, and on September 25, 1918 two months later General Bandholtz replaced Groome.

When General Pershing sent for Harry, he stated, "Now, Bandholtz, you are going to hate me for this. But the Provost Department is in a disgraceful condition. I want you to take hold of it and put it in shape. When you can come to me and say that the provost guard is working to your satisfaction, you can go back to your command at the front." Harry was deeply saddened by the loss of his battlefield command, but accepted this new challenge. The war ended with him still in place as Provost Marshal General.[101]

In "Origins of the Military Police", Jacob B. Lishchiner states, "officers and enlisted men performing military police duties, were to wear a blue brassard halfway up the left arm, between the elbow and shoulder, bearing the letters M.P. in white." According to the Quartermaster Museum, the "official" brassard was made from a blue denim material, the letters outlined in white stitching. A variety of actual brassards have been reported, many locally produced by

---

[101] *Jungle Patrol*

military police organizations. However, the "Regulations for the Provost Marshal General's Department, AEF," dated December 9, 1917, state the brassard was to be blue with red lettering. These regulations further state, "The plain-clothes officer investigates, and if necessary arrests, frequently with the help of the uniform branch, all cases which lie below the surface, while the uniform officer deals mostly with what takes place openly and in the sight of all." This is the only reference to an "investigative arm" of the Provost Marshal General's Department, and nowhere are the duties of criminal investigators described.

The regulations go on to outline the myriad tasks of Military Police. They were responsible for the direction of motor traffic, moving supplies from embarkation areas to forward operating bases, as well as overseeing troop marches to round up stragglers and or deserters. Security of depot areas, the detection and investigation of theft, and any other crimes committed by or against the Army. MPs were called upon to safeguard private citizens and their property from looters or other marauding soldiers. Offending soldiers often had to be confined, and their custody was an MP function. During and immediately after the war, prisoners of war had to be treated according to international treaties, so stockades, or prisoner of war camps were built and manned by members of the Provost Marshal General's Department.

Harry was the first Provost Marshal General who had any type of police training or experience, based on his time with the constabulary. The same was true of the junior officers and enlisted men. Although the need for military police was universally recognized and thousands of men were performing military police functions throughout the Army, the pressing need for their services left selection of personnel haphazard and specialized professional training limited. Former policemen were recruited whenever possible and placed in training positions. Studies were made of British Military Police organizations and functions. A US model was based on those findings.

During the early stages of American involvement in the war, the prime concern was getting troops and their equipment to the front. Each division was entitled to two military police companies, and the Commander of Trains served the additional duty as Division Provost Marshal. Stationary posts were established at major intersections, to enable the convoys to be given priority, while other MPs rode motorcycles as escorts, or to scout the road ahead. In those days, traffic consisted of motor vehicles, horse or mule drawn vehicles, men afoot, or on horseback. Many roads were dirt and soon became rivers of mud, or were badly rutted by the wagon wheels.

US Army Engineers road-building, US Army Photo

In a letter home, dated July 2, 1918, Corporal Norris Ball, a steamroller operator, Company E, 23$^{rd}$ Engineers, wrote to his brother in Colorado, regarding the terrible condition of the roads in France and the poor machinery they had for road improvement. Most of the roads in his area were deeply rutted by the animal drawn carts of the native population, and the French machinery was in poor condition for doing major road repairs. The coal used to fuel the steam engines of the rollers was described, "they have the poorest coal over here, I ever used, being the slack from the mines compressed into oval shaped bricketts (sic) the size of an egg, and being mostly slate."[102]

The heavy Army trucks took their toll on the inadequate road surfaces. The military police trying to get convoys to the front had a monumental task.

As fighting progressed, and prisoners captured, they had to be transported to the safety of the rear areas. This too was a responsibility of the military police. Confinement camps were constructed and guards trained to properly care for prisoners of war.

Congress finally authorized the establishment of a Military Police Corps, on October 15, 1918. This new corps was to consist of the Provost Marshal General Department- AEF, all military police units in the AEF, and all "additional personnel." Harry re-organized the entire Provost Marshal's Department. The result was a Military Police Corps superior in numbers to any law enforcement organization of that time. In area the department covered the countries of the British Isles, France, Belgium, Luxembourg, Italy, and the occupied portions of Germany and Austria. Under his command were 1,405 officers and 40,670 enlisted men. He was also responsible for the care of 48,380 German prisoners of war captured by the American Forces.

The standards for Military Police were established as: all personnel must be 21 years of age, or older; at least 5 feet 7 inches in height with proportionate weight; free of all physical defects; be able to read and write English well and speak the language fluently; be intelligent and not addicted to liquor. A military police private must possess all the qualities required of a non-commissioned officer. The military policeman was also to receive a pay incentive with privates given the assimilated grade of lance corporal.

---

[102] *Personal letter of Corporal Norris Ball*

"Espirit de corps must be cultivated to the maximum limit. The members of the organization must be made to feel that theirs is the elite organization and that there are no more important responsibilities than theirs."

"The Military Police are concerned with all crimes and offenses committed within the area of the organization to which attached, but in exercising their power they must act with judgment and discretion. While they must assert their authority whenever necessary, and must not hesitate to report violations of, or refusal to obey, orders issued by them in the performance of their duties, they must do so in a quiet dignified manner, free from overbearingness or abuse. In short, good sense, self-restraint and courtesy must govern the Military Police in exercising their authority."[103]

To distinguish them, the uniform of the officers and enlisted men of the Military Police Corps will be the same as that of other members of the American Expeditionary Forces with the following exceptions: Enlisted men will wear service hats, with a plain one-inch wide red band, or a strip of red cloth attached to the overseas cap, if the service hat is not available. All ranks will wear a strip of red cloth, 2 inches long and 1-1/4 inches wide, rounded at the corners, sewn on the collar lengthwise, one inch from each end of their collar and midway between the upper and lower edges of the collar, with the regulation "U.S.," in the case of officers, and with the regulation button collar insignia, in the case of enlisted men superimposed on center."[104]

A new Provost Marshal General's Manual was written, outlining the duties of each of the sections, such as Organization of the Department, Prisoner of War Escort Companies, Prisoner of War Labor Companies, Inspectors/Instructors, Traffic Control, Details of Highway

---

[103] *Military Police and Constabulary*, by BG Harry H. Bandholtz, Bandholtz Papers.
[104] *Manual for the Provost Marshal General's Department, A.E.F.*, dated 1919, Printing Office, G.P.B., A.E.F.

Motorcycle Patrols, Criminal Investigation Division, Passes and Permits, Reports and Returns.

The Provost Marshal General's Department was to be comprised of one general officer, one colonel, 10 lieutenant colonels, 30 majors, 70 captains, 10 first lieutenants and 10 second lieutenants. In addition there was one regimental sergeant major, 2 battalion sergeants major, 4 sergeants, 4 corporals, 20 enlisted men, and 12 field clerks. This would be amended in a matter of weeks.

The basic organizational unit remained the Military Police Company, which as of October 1918 consisted of 205 officers and men. Each division was allotted one of these larger military police companies, in lieu of the two formerly used. Equipment for the AEF Company was listed in the new manual. Including 50 riding horses, 6 mules, 1 wagon, 18 motorcycles, and 105 bicycles, it was one of the most mobile organizations in the Army. Military Police on duty were to be armed with a club and a pistol.[105]

BG H. H. Bandholtz, center, with his Staff, France
Bandholtz Papers, UMICH

---

[105] Ibid

A Military Police Training Center was established at Autun, France, during the last months of the war. It trained and graduated over 4,000 officers and men during its brief existence. The Commandant and Chief Instructor of this school was Lieutenant Colonel Harvey L. Jones. Jones had been Inspector General of the 29$^{th}$ Division, the same unit Harry had served with.[106] Nevertheless, familiar patterns continued to persist. Men, usually with no experience in such duties, were drafted out of other units and thrust into military police organizations where they were expected to learn on the job.

Requisitions had been made, for the formation of Military Police Battalions, in French speaking areas of the United States (namely New England and Louisiana), emphasizing the need for personnel with police experience.

With the end of hostilities, Paris became a haven for soldiers no longer fighting an enemy. It was a city of recreation and relaxation and seemed like every woman had a soldier beside her. The war wounded on crutches or walking with canes could be seen leading those who were blind, or had their faces bandaged. Many criminals prowled the streets to relieve the able bodied and recovering wounded from their paychecks. Prostitutes were everywhere, and the outbreak of venereal disease was widespread. Robbers also took their toll by attacking soldiers and taking their valuables, frequently resulting in the murder of the victim.

In a letter dated November 29, 1918, Pershing wrote to Harry, "It gives me great pleasure to inform you that on October 17$^{th}$ I recommended you for promotion to the grade of Major General, basing my recommendation upon the efficiency of your service with the American Expeditionary Forces." However, this same letter goes on to state, "The War Department discontinued all promotions of General

---

[106] *"History of the 29th Division," by John A. Cutchins, Press of MacCalla & Co, Philadelphia 1921, pg 246*

Officers after the signing of the Armistice, and I regret that you will not therefore receive the deserved recognition of your excellent services."

In a memorandum to Harry, dated December 21, 1918, the Provost Marshal of Paris, Lieutenant Colonel John C. White, described the terrible condition of the Military Police of Paris. He describes the living conditions of the $201^{st}$ Military Police Company, being billeted in an old hotel with troops of other disciplines, and also with 50 to 100 prisoners pending transfer to a local jail. The crowded situations in Paris, and other cities would only be relieved as the majority of troops were boarded for the voyage home.

In an effort to calm the city, the Commanding General of the District of Paris, enacted a curfew ordering all enlisted men off the streets by 9 PM. Against the wishes of the Provost Marshal, he also ordered all his staff officers to serve as assistant provost marshals (APM), wearing the brassard and making arrests. The Provost Marshal of Paris, Colonel White, objected stating that "Officers thus appointed lack experience in A.P.M. work, make arrests without judgment and interfere with proper Military Police." The matter was resolved and the order was rescinded.

January of 1919 saw a change in the configuration of the Provost Marshal General's Department, adding new positions and personnel. On March 31, 1919, Harry, in a memorandum to General Pershing, requested the establishment of a permanent Military Police Corps, and subsequently put it into a draft proposal for an Act of Congress. The proposal was not favorably considered. The Congressional Library was unable to locate a Bill of this nature, during the time frame concerned.

On March 28, 1919, from his headquarters in France, General Pershing wrote a personal letter to Harry in which he stated, "It is my desire at this time to express to the officers and men of the Provost Marshal General's Department an appreciation of the services they have rendered during the period of active hostilities and since the signing of the armistice. The duties of the Department, especially of the Military Police Corps, consisting as they have of the enforcement of law and order, the control of traffic and circulation, the custody of prisoners of war, the apprehension of absentees and the recovery of stolen property have been of an especially trying and onerous nature. Working under difficult conditions in a strange country whose laws and customs differed fundamentally from their own, they have succeeded in maintaining the best of relations with the civilian population and in all respects upholding the good name of their countrymen. From the base ports to the firing line they have represented the American Government and its laws to the mutual benefit and well-being of all concerned."

In his final report on the war, dated 1920, General Pershing wrote to the Secretary of War, "The military police of the American Expeditionary Forces developed into one of the most striking bodies of men in Europe. Wherever the American soldier went, there our military police were on duty. They controlled traffic in the battle zone, in all villages occupied by American troops, and in many cities through which our traffic flowed; they maintained order, so far as the American soldier was concerned; throughout France and in portions of England, Italy, Belgium, and occupied Germany. Their smart appearance and military bearing and the intelligent manner in which they discharged their duties left an excellent impression of the typical American on all with whom they came into contact."[107]

---

[107] *Final Report of Gen. John J. Pershing, 1920, Government Printing Office*

General Pershing addressing General Bandholtz (extreme left) and the PMG Staff, with permission, Military Police Museum

In view of the rapid dissolution of the American Expeditionary Forces, Pershing called a conference of Chiefs of Divisions of the General Staff, to determine the means of and dates for a gradual decrease in personnel of administrative and staff departments until changing conditions and circumstances would permit them eventually and finally returning to cease functioning altogether.[108] As a result of this meeting, it closed the existence of the Provost Marshal General's Department as a part of the American Expeditionary Forces.

---

[108] *G.H.Q. American Expeditionary Forces General Orders No. 84. France, May 27, 1919. Closing of Provost Marshal General's Office at Chaumont*

# Chapter Fifteen

## DIVISION OF CRIMINAL INVESTIGATION

LTC Edwin O. Saunders
Used by permission of his daughter

Some sources say the birth of an Army criminal investigation division took place during the US Civil War or even earlier. However it was not until World War I that a military unit, composed of regular soldiers, was assigned to criminal investigative duties. There were certainly civilian investigators during the Civil War, but these were primarily involved in intelligence operations, or enforcement of draft laws.

It was May 11, 1918, that General Pershing ordered the formation of a Division of Criminal Investigation (DCI), under the direction of an officer "who possesses a thorough knowledge of detective work in all of its branches and who will be the technical advisor of the Provost Marshal General on all questions arising from criminal investigation work," This order remained virtually ignored until much later. In November 1918, Pershing directed his fourth Provost Marshal General, Harry Bandholtz, "A criminal investigation division be organized by the Provost Marshal General from the Military Police Corps and the attached commissioned and enlisted personnel, to which may be added a number of civilian operatives at such rates of pay and allowances as the Commander in Chief may from time to time authorize."

On December 12, 1918, Harry appointed a Judge Advocate's Division Officer, Lieutenant Colonel Edwin O. Saunders[109] to establish the D.C.I. This very capable man, a 1912 graduate of the University of Buffalo Law School, formed an organization of seven Criminal Investigation Companies to cover P.M.G. Headquarters, the three Armies, the City of Paris, and all the Base Sections.[110] Another company of operatives, commanded by Captain Karl W. Detzer,[111] was added to cover the Embarkation Center, LeMans, France, and a detachment from Headquarters covered the British Isles. D.C.I. Companies were authorized five officers and 100 "operatives," however these numbers varied as the missions were formulated. Those of Paris and Bordeaux, at times, had 150 operatives, while others like Le Mans had a considerably smaller number. On February 5, 1919, under General Order #5, A.E.F. the eight D.C.I. units were designated, as the 301 (Bordeux), 302 (St. Nazaire), 303 Brest), 304 (Neufchateau), 305 (Nevers), 306 (Paris), 307 (at large), and (for LeMans) the 308th MP Companies (Criminal Investigation). The 307th Company was divided into four detachments, one being assigned to each of the three field armies, and the fourth assuming responsibility for the Provost Marshal General's Headquarters. The headquarters

---

[109] *Edwin O. Saunder, (1878-1966), Col., JAGC, US Army*

[110] *Base Sections were re-supply depots where a 45-day of supplies were stored,. These were located at various locations in France. Some also housed replacement soldiers.*

[111] *Karl W. Detzer, (1891-1987), Col, GS, US Army*

detachment was further sub-divided with a group assigned to London. D.C.I. Operatives had the authority to travel anywhere in the theater and conducted investigations in Belgium, occupied Germany, Italy, or wherever criminal activity was taking place. This order also authorized the wearing of civilian clothes, and the carrying of special passes to allow investigators access to any area. They were armed mostly with the US Model 1911 Semi Automatic Pistol, of .45 caliber. Shoulder holsters were issued for concealed carry while in civilian attire.

As a tribute to their commander, the internal newsletter of the DCI, Paris, included a cartoon of Colonel Saunders. It was accompanied by a ditty outlining his attributes.

*"He's got an eye keener than that of a Malay diver fishing for pearls and he can see through more clouds and verbal camouflage that ever dripped from the prolific pen of Conan Doyle. The Colonel is full of deductive processes and inductive syllograms, he savies all the psychological bunk about psychopathic phenomena and he knows a hawk from a handsaw."*

Pourpoi Newsletter, DCI Paris, March 1919

The D.C.I. was charged with the investigation of crimes committed by or against members of the United States Forces. It was soon determined that the draft brought into the military many criminals or profiteers. With large quantities of supplies stored in various areas, it became lucrative for those bent on making money, to tap into these resources, steal what they could and sell it on the black-market. For example, two enlisted men, from the 58$^{th}$ Infantry, posing as officers, hired a band of foreign nationals for their thievery. They ultimately became personnel of interest to operatives of the D.C.I. who recovered over 21,000 francs, the proceeds from sales of the stolen property, in addition to a motorcycle. The two men were arrested and the foreign nationals turned over to French authorities.

Another case, investigated by the Paris Office, involved a gang of deserters who committed larcenies, robberies, sexual assaults, etc. In January 1919, a concerted effort was made to locate and identify these men. On the 29$^{th}$ of the month, a raid was conducted and nine men arrested. The arrest is alleged to have occurred after a fierce gun battle with the criminals. Large sums of cash, guns of various types and calibers, officer's uniforms and equipment were recovered, along with a Red Cross Ambulance loaded with loot from a railroad baggage room

A soldier, who also became a man of interest of D.C.I. Nazaire, was Corporal Allen J. Wilson, 309$^{th}$ Engineers. He was questioned but would not admit involvement in criminal activity. He did confess that he enlisted in the Army under false pretenses. He was fingerprinted, photographed, and the investigation continued. Through these efforts it was learned Wilson was in fact William Lustgarten, an embezzler wanted by New York Police. He had faked his own suicide, changed identity and enlisted in the army. Lustgarten was returned to New York and turned over to civil police.

On July 31, 1919, the Brooklyn Daily Standard Newspaper, which had been covering the trial, published the following article in their court section:

*"LUSTGARTEN CONVICTED OF $20,000 SWINDLE*

*A jury before Judge CRAIN, in General Sessions, Manhattan, to-day found William LUSTGARTEN guilty of fleecing New Yorkers out of a large sum of money. It is said the total amount of the losses of men who invested in the Tax Lien Company will amount to $800,000, but the specific charge against LUSTGARTEN was getting away with $20,000 belonging to Robert SCHALKENBACH.*

*LUSTGARTEN disappeared in August 1917, after leaving a bundle of clothes and a suicide note on a pier. He was later recognized at an army unit by two young women. He enlisted under the name of Allan H. WILSON and after serving in many camps was sent to France, where he was arrested.*

*Among LUSTGARTEN's victims are F. LEUBUSCHER, Frank L. MONTAGUE, ex-City Chamberlain Milo R. MALTBIO, ex-Dock Commissioner Calvin TOMKINS and John MARTIN. The money was invested to buy real estate, which was never purchased. "*

The Provost Marshal General's Report, for 1919, states that during the period December 12, 1918 - April 12, 1919, over 4,500 cases were handled by the D.C.I. Of these, 23 were highway robbery, 32 were murders, and there were 25 instances of rape. The remainder included cases of theft, assault, and black market activities. Members of the D.C.I received many letters of commendation.

In March of 1919, a new "Manual for the Provost Marshal General's Department, AEF," was published. This monumental book describes the functions of the Criminal Investigation Division (CID), the organization of its units and their duties. It also provides for CID Credentials, civilian clothing allowances, availability of separate rations and housing allowances when required for an investigation. It

accused of. Colonel Saunders traveled from Chic
testify on behalf of his former subordinate. The trial en
acquittal of all charges and Detzer was allowed to con
his military career, retiring after World War II.

also states, "Except in cases where specially ordered to do so, members of the Military Police Corps on criminal investigation work shall not wear the prescribed brassard, red hat band, nor any other mark or insignia exposing their identity as members of the Military Police Corps."

Only one reference has been found indicating a casualty among the D.C.I. Units. A black undercover operative, from the Brest Office, was posing as a stevedore. During September 1919, while he was trying to arrest criminals he was overpowered and murdered.[112]

With this firm foundation, it must have been heartbreaking for those involved when the D.C.I. was transferred to Headquarters, Services and Supply, on May 28, 1919 and the MP Corps was dissolved just days later. It would not be until World War II when there would be a reintroduction of CID units.

Upon their return to the United States many of the returning soldiers had been discharged and allowed to go home. Others were subjected to additional service, due to unforeseen circumstances. One particular incident would cast a dark shadow on the Military Police Corps, and the D.C.I., in particular.

Captain Karl W. Detzer, Commanding Officer of the 308th MP Company, had been brought up on charges of prisoner abuse, by a couple of miscreants arrested by members of his unit. As a result, Detzer faced a General Court Martial, charged with 28 counts of misconduct. The trial, conducted at Governor's Island (later Fort Jay), New York, during December 1919, lasted several weeks. Witnesses were heard testifying against the actions of Captain Detzer, accusing him of brutality. The allegations were supported by some of the members of his former unit. In his defense, others were called who stated he had been a fair man, and regulations in place to prevent the type actions he

---

[112] *True Tales of the D.C.I.*, Karl Detzer, Bobbs-Merrill, 1925,

# Chapter Sixteen
# HUNGARY

General Bandholtz was relieved of his position as Provost Marshal General in August 1919 and reassigned as the American Representative on the Inter-Allied Military Mission to Hungary. These missions were developed by the Allied Supreme Council, and were designed to observe and report on the obedience to provisions of the Treaty of Versailles. While they did have a certain amount of authority, they were generally without sufficient troops to enforce the regulations. This mission to Hungary was to consist of general officers from the United States, Great Britain, Italy and France, along with their supporting staffs. His orders read:

*American Commission To Negotiate Peace, Paris,*

*August 6, 1919*

*Brigadier General H. H. Bandholtz, U.S. A.,*

*Paris, France.*

*By direction of the American Commissioners I have to inform you that you have been named the American representative on the Inter-Allied Military Mission to Hungary, established by the Supreme Council of the Peace Conference. A copy of the instructions to the Mission as agreed upon by the Council is enclosed herewith for your information and guidance.*

*I am, Sir,*

*Your obedient servant*

*[signed]*

*Diplomatic Secretary*[113]

---

[113] *Bandholtz Diaries, Hungarian National Museum*

The other generals received their orders through the Supreme Command of the Allied Armies, and were signed by General Weyand,[114] Chief of Staff for Marshal Foch.[115] In the case of British General Gorton, the orders addressed to General Sackville-West, British Military Delegate to the Peace Conference read: "At its meeting of $5^{th}$ August, the Supreme Council of the Peace Conference appointed General Gorton as British Representative of the Inter-Allied Commission which is to proceed to Budapest. As General Gorton is at present at Presburg, I should be obliged if you would kindly notify him of this appointment and forward him the instructions issued by the conference, a copy of which you will find enclosed."

The enclosed instructions included: "The object of the Mission will be to get into communication with the Hungarian Government in order that observance of the armistice may be assured and all disarmament effectively carried out."[116] This was going to be much more difficult than in other countries, where similar missions were being sent. At war's end, the government of Hungary was in disarray. The weakened hierarchy fell and a Communist Regime took control.

The Hungarian Soviet Republic, formed early in the year 1919, was led by Bela Kun (Bela Kohn), who was born in Transylvania, on February 20, 1886. Serving in Hungary's armed forces during the war, Kun was captured and imprisoned by the Russian Bolsheviks. It was in Moscow, November 1918, where he and other Hungarian prisoners-of-war, along with Communist sympathizers, formed a Central Committee, for a Hungarian Communist Party. Upon his return to Hungary, he took control of the Communist Party, and subsequently took over the government.

---

[114] *Maxime Weygand ( 1867-1965)was a French military commander in World War I*
[115] *Marshal Ferdinand Foch (October 2, 1851 – March 20, 1929), of France, Supreme Commander of Allied Forces during the Great War*
[116] *Gorton Papers, British Public Records Office, Kew*

During his regime, his Hungarian Red Army attacked Czech forces, which had taken control of some northern Hungarian cities. This was stopped by an Allied ultimatum that Kun was to evacuate all reclaimed territory. Simultaneously, the Hungarian Red Army was fighting Romanian troops in the Tisza River Valley. The poorly disciplined Hungarians were ordered into a general retreat, unable to withstand the Romanian Army's advance. Kun's government was short lived, lasting only a few months. In this short time, however, the losses to Hungary were greater than during all of the World War.

Being a part of the Austria-Hungary Empire, and an enemy of the allies, this ancient civilization was treated badly by the victors. After the war had ended, the Czechs on one side, and Romania on another, attacked and occupied parts of Hungary. Their attacks were to topple the Kun government. With the defeat and exile of Bela Kun, Romanian forces moved into and occupied Budapest, installing a Socialist Democratic Government. Almost immediately they started confiscating materials and equipment, in violation of rules established by the Peace Commission

It was into this confused and unstable situation, that Harry made his appearance. With orders in hand, he started out by rail, from Paris to Budapest, at just after 9AM, on August 7.

He and his party were traveling with Mr. Herbert Hoover, head of the American Relief Administration, in the latter's private rail car. The rest of Harry's staff would follow as quickly as possible. This would consist of ten officers and twenty-five enlisted soldiers, some of who served with him in France.

General Bandholtz and Staff in Budapest
with permission, Hungarian National Museum

To assist him in this endeavor, Harry brought along Colonel James T. Loree,[117] of the Quartermaster Department, his Assistant Executive Officer, and an expert in railroad operations. He also brought Colonel Raymond Sheldon and his personal aide, Captain E. B. Gore. The following morning, shortly after crossing into Switzerland, the party was held for five hours. Some were not in possession of passports, and the Swiss were insisting that no one travel in their country wearing a military uniform. Bandholtz was able to borrow a blue coat from Hoover, a tie from his stenographer, and a golf cap from another. Removal of his spurs completed what he refers to in his diary as "demobilization." Once Harry and his aide, Captain Gore,[118] had civilianized themselves, the Swiss finally agreed they could travel in uniform under escort of a Swiss policeman, who would accompany them all the way to the Austrian Border. They arrived at the town of Buchs, near the frontier line, about six o'clock P.M., when Captain Gregory,[119] Mr.

---

[117] *James Tabor Loree, grew up in the railroad business, his father being President of the Delaware and Hudson Railroad, and CEO of the Eastern Division of the Railroad War Board. James was a graduate of Yale University, and chose the military as a career.*
[118] *Captain Edwin Bulkley Gore, Member US Mission*
[119] *Captain Thomas C. Gregory, US Food Administrator in Vienna,*

Hoover's representative in Austria, joined them. After an hour, they proceeded on their journey. On August 9th, in Linz, Austria, the parties separated, Mr. Hoover continuing on to Warsaw, Poland and the Bandholtz group taking a train via Vienna to Budapest.

As conquerors, the Romanians felt they were entitled to whatever they could remove from Hungary. Marie, Queen of Romania, had even written to Herbert Hoover, American delegate[120] to the treaty of Versailles, "Romania was being treated as the enemy whilst the enemy was treated as a friend," arguing that her soldiers were only taking from Hungary things that had been stolen from Romania during the war. At an earlier time, Marie, in agreeing to an alliance,[121] August 17, 1916, stated she wanted the lands of Transylvania ceded to Romania, as her price for cooperation.[122]

On August 7, 1919, the Peace Conference was informed that Archduke Joseph, former regent of Hungary, had retaken his seat, through a bloodless coup d'etat.[123] Four days later, on his first day in Budapest, Harry met with his British counterpart, Brigadier Reginald St. George Gorton,[124] a former intelligence officer and they discussed the organization of the Mission. The two then received the

---

[120] *For his efforts, he became an important wartime adviser to President Woodrow Wilson, who made Hoover a part of the American delegation to the conference of the Treaty of Versailles.*
[121] *The Romanian government signed a treaty with the Allies on August 17, 1916 and declared war on the Central Powers on August 27.*
[122] *The Last Romantic-Life of Marie, Queen of Roumania, Hannah Pakula*
[123] *NY Times, Archduke Seizes Power in Hungary, Aug 8, 1919*
[124] *General Gorton (1866-1944) was born in Lincolnshire, England. At age 20 he entered the British Army's Royal Artillery and served in the 1891 Miranzai Expedition and the Chitral Campaign of 1895. During 1899-1903 he served in the South African War and in Europe during WWI. He retired from military service in 1922, returning to Lincolshire with his wife Dorothea, until his death.*

Archduke Joseph,[125] temporary head of the Hungarian Republic. During the war, the Archduke had commanded first a division, and then a corps on the Italian front, and was thought of as a capable military leader. On the 27th of October 1918 Kaiser Karl[126] appointed Joseph as "Homo regius" (King's vassal) for Hungary. Joseph requested of the Kaiser to be released from his oath of allegiance. He immediately started negotiations towards the building of a new national government on October 29. 1918. However, these efforts were destroyed by the outbreak of the communist revolution two days later. During the short lived Communist republic, Joseph was held under observation on his estate at Alcsuth. He was so popular that not even the Bolsheviks would risk harming him more than this. After the collapse of the red revolution he again took over the function of head of state with the title Regent, he appointed Istvan Friedrich as Prime Minister and confirmed Admiral Nikolaus von Horthy[127] as supreme commander of the Hungarian National Army. Joseph never made any secret of his plan to get the legal monarch Kaiser Karl back to the throne of Hungary and consequently the Entente Powers finally forced him to abdicate and hand over power to Friedrich. He did not completely retire from politics and when the House of Lords was installed again in 1927 he became a member of that institution.

---

[125] *Joseph August Viktor Klemens Maria, Archduke of Austria, Prince of Hungary and Bohemia (9 August 1872 – 6 July 1962),*
[126] *Karl Franz Josef von Habsburg-Lothringen, Emperor of Austria-Hungary*
[127] *Miklos Horthy was born in Kenderes, Hungary, on June 18 1868, to a wealthy noble family. He was educated at the Naval Academy, in Fiume, Hungary, and upon graduation was appointed sub-lieutenant. With various assignments before, and during the war, Horthy was promoted to Admiral in February of 1918, and named Commander in Chief of the Fleet. At war's end he returned to his family home, in Kenderes, which had been looted first by the Hungarian Bolshevists and again by the Romanians.*

troops in Budapest, and General Gheorghe D. Mardarescu,[131] Commander-in-Chief of the Romanian Army.

General Gorton, presiding, accepted their agreement to take steps to ease the famine conditions, which were rampant in the city, and their wish to cooperate fully with the Military Mission. Mr. Diamandi met privately later with General Bandholtz, and apologized for his behavior of the previous day.

Believing the Mission would be a short-term operation; the American Peace Commission authorized General Bandholtz a staff of three officers and twenty-five enlisted men. As it turned out, this was not nearly enough, and additional officers were detailed to him. The enlisted men were not an organized unit, but randomly assigned. However, Harry was gratified to learn that each was an "experienced Military Policeman."[132]

---

[131] *Gheorghe Mardarescu was born on 4 August 1866 in Iasi, Romania. He graduated the Infantry and Cavalry Officer School in Bucharest in 1888 and between 1892-1894 he attended the Military Academy and then command courses in Brueck and Spandau. Between 1901-1906 he was the director of studies at the Military Academy. He then commanded the Infantry Firing School and was Chief of Staff for the 1st and then the 2nd Corps. In 1915 he was appointed commander of the Military Academy. After 15 August 1916, Mardarescu received the command of the 18th Infantry Brigade. At the end of the month he was appointed Chief of Staff of the 3rd Army, commanded by the future marshal Alexandru Averescu. When general Averescu took over the 2nd Army in September of that year, he brought along his chief of staff. Mardarescu remained in this position also during the heavy battles of 1917, in which the 2nd Army played an important role. In February 1918 he was promoted to major general and became the Technical Inspector of the Infantry. Mardarescu remained in this position until 11 April 1919, when he was appointed commander of the Romanian troops in Transylvania. After the war he was the Minister of Defense for four years. In 1927 he was promoted to the rank of Lieutenant General. Gheorghe Mardarescu passed away on 5 September 1938 in Neuheimbad, Germany.*
[132] *Final Report of the Mission, Bandholtz Papers, Hungarian National Museum*

General Bandholtz again presided over the Mission on August 16<sup>th</sup>. On that date he read a telegram from the Supreme Council, and also the draft of a proposal he thought should be presented to the Romanians. This was agreed to, and the Romanian Commander in Chief, along with his chief of staff were informed the Romanians were to:

1: (a) Cease at once requisitioning or taking possession of any supplies or property of whatever nature except in zones authorized by this Mission, and then only of such supplies as may be necessary for the Romanian Army, and that this Mission be informed as to the kind of supplies which will be considered necessary.

(b) The Romanian Commander in Chief to furnish without delay a map clearly showing the requisition zones, and also indicating thereon the disposition of his troops.

(c) Return at once to its owners all private property then in the possession of the Romanians, such as automobiles, horses, carriages, or any other property of which the ownership is vested in individuals.

(d) To arrange for the gradual return to the Hungarian Government of the railroad, post and telegraph systems.

(e) Make no further requisitions of buildings, stores or real property and evacuate as rapidly as possible all schools, colleges, and buildings of like character.

(f) Cease at once all shipments of rolling stock or Hungarian property of any kind whatsoever, to or towards Romania, and stop and return to Budapest any rolling stock or property already en route or held at outside stations.

(g) Limit supervision over public or private affairs in the city to such extent as may be approved by this Mission.

2: The Romanian government was to furnish this Mission not later than August twenty-third a complete list of all war material, railway or agricultural material, live stock or property of any kind whatsoever that has been taken possession of, in Hungary by Romanian forces.[133]

Harry noted, "They were also given a few more bitter pills which they swallowed with apparent complacency. I wired the American Mission in Paris this evening that in my opinion the Romanians were doing their utmost to delay matters in order to complete the loot of Hungary and that as far as I could see their progress up to date in complying with the Supreme Council's desires, was negative rather than positive."

The morning's session, of August 19th, Harry again presiding, was one of the most interesting. The Hungarian Minister of War was introduced and submitted a verbal proposition for the reorganization of the Hungarian Army. He was told to reduce the same to writing and submit it without delay. A complaint was received that the Hungarians have been making arrests and committing abuses in certain districts which had been assigned by the Peace Conference to Austria, and it was decided to ask the Supreme Council to give a clarification of the present geographical limits of Hungary.

Next, Constantin Diamandi came in with the Romanian General Mardarescu, and a new star in the Romanian constellation in the person of a General Rudeanu. Mardarescu was put on the carpet and told in strong terms that it was his responsibility to report what had been done to comply with the orders of August 16, 1919. Harry observed, "He resorted to all sorts of evasions and circumlocutions, which may have been intentional or may have been due to his grade of intelligence, which appears to be about that of a comatose caribou." Diamandi insisted that in the future, whenever matters of importance were discussed with a Hungarian official, the Romanian government should be represented. His proposition was laid on the table and he

---

[133] *Bandholtz Diaries, Hungarian National Museum*

received no reply, as the commission proposed to use its own judgment in regard to such matters.

During that afternoon, General Rudeanu privately visited General Bandholtz, in his office, stating that his intentions were honorable and that he would see the orders of the Mission were carried out. This, however, turned out to be another ploy! The looting continued and stolen goods were being assembled in various transportation centers.

Later in August 1919, the Archduke resigned and turned over control of his government, preferably to the Allied Commission. His cabinet was immediately informed the Commission had no authority, nor desire, to establish a new Hungarian Government, and it was their responsibility to do so. The Archduke then appointed one Istvan Friedrich, a long time politician, as Prime Minister of the new government.

Problems persisted with the Romanian Army and their reluctance to abide by the rules set down by the Allied Commission. On August 27th, a British Army Major reported that at Szolnok, roughly 100 miles east of Budapest, he located rolling stock, consisting of 150 locomotives, 200 to 300 empty freight cars, 4 airplanes (on cars), 200 to 300 tank cars, and many hundreds of carloads of merchandise, loaded by the Romanians, waiting to cross the bridge towards Romania. The Romanians continue to insist that they are only recovering material taken from them during the war. However, it was learned they had been stripping warehouses of freight car loads of shoes, and clothing, and gutting factories and hospitals of their equipment and supplies.

A split can also been seen developing within the Commission, the French and Italian delegates catering to the Romanians, while the American and British were insisting that Romania leave Hungary as quickly as possible.

On the personal side of things, Harry Bandholtz was living the luxurious life; with a residence and office located within the fabulous royal palace, on the grounds of Buda Castle, perched on the heights overlooking the River Danube. He had a staff to cook delicious meals, and the Royal Box at the Opera. In fact, he had three boxes, one for himself, and the others for staff and guests. He frequently writes that it will be difficult going back to life as an average American. However, there are times when he is shocked into "reality."

Buda Castle, Residence and Office of Gen. Bandholtz
photo by author

On September 7th, he and members of his staff departed Budapest on a special train, in a special car, provided by the King of Romania. He had been invited by the King to visit the Royal Palace, in Sinaia, Romania, the King's summer residence. That night he slept on a hair filled mattress. General Bandholtz wrote in his diary, "because the hairs pushed up through the mattress, through the sheets and through my pajamas, and could be very distinctly felt. In addition to this, the mattress undoubtedly had a large and animated population." He relates that this was not only for his benefit, but all of his companions had the same experience. He further writes, "Last night, while traveling through eastern Hungary, we saw large numbers of cars loaded with stuff, all en route to Roumania (sic)."

This particular trip was an official visit to the Romanian Royal Family, situated in the Carpathian Mountains about seventy-five miles north of Bucharest, the capital. King

Carol I, of Romania, built the 70-room residence[134] for his nephew and heir, Ferdinand, on the grounds of an earlier, and larger royal residence. The reasons for the visit were an attempt to convince the General that the Romanians were not being treated as Allies, but rather like thieves. The newspapers of the day indicate the Allied Peace Commission, in Paris, did not send him to Bucharest and even suggest that he acted on his own. In any case, the Romanian Royal Family provided the special train and accommodations. He and his staff were billeted within the Royal Palace.

At dinner that evening, General Bandholtz was seated to the left of King Ferdinand, a seat of honor. In an after dinner discussion with the King, Bandholtz was invited into his private office, where the conversation continued. The King related Romanian grievances, with special attention being pointed out that they were being considered robbers, because of the looting of Hungary, while others were not called onto the carpet for their looting. He also brought up other matters that were not within the realm of responsibilities of the Allied Commission. Harry courteously explained the Inter-Allied Military Mission had explicit instructions on what was to happen in Hungary, and that he was not in a position to discuss the matter further. He also stated that he had planned to return to Budapest the following morning.

The King insisted that Harry stay at least until noon because his wife, the Queen, wished to meet the General. As a matter of fact, he did not have to insist, because transportation away from Sinaia was entirely at the King's disposition, and no one could leave until he saw fit to let him go.

---

[134] *Pelisor Castle was built in 1899–1903 by order of King Carol I, as the residence for his nephew and heir, the future King Ferdinand (son of Carol's brother Leopold von Hohenzollern) and Ferdinand's consort Queen Marie.*

Her Majesty, Marie, Queen of Romania
by permission, Hungarian National Museum

With the discussions with the King completed, Harry retired to his assigned quarters within the palace. The rooms were much more comfortable than his compartment on the train, and he was able to get a good night's rest. His staff also looked more relaxed when they assembled in the morning. They arrived for breakfast at about 8.30, and met Her Majesty, the Queen, and one of the Royal Princesses. Queen Marie,[135] of Romania was English born, and a former Princess of Edinburgh. Her Majesty was wearing the Roumanian (sic) peasant costume, which was very becoming, and she was decidedly a handsome woman, showing that she must have been beautiful when younger. The Royal aide-de-camp informed Harry that he was to sit at the left of Madame Simky Lahovary, one of the ladies in waiting. So he entered the dining room in that order. However, immediately after he entered, the Queen called out from the head of the table, "General, I want you to sit up by me." So Harry, in his words, "in fear and trembling", approached the Royal presence and sat on her left, with the King on her right. Without any preliminaries, Her Majesty

---

[135] *Marie was the daughter of Alfred Ernest Albert, Duke of Edinburgh and Grand-Duchess <u>Marie Alexandrovna</u> of Russia, therefore a grand daughter of Queen Victoria, of England, and Tsar Alexander II, of Russia.*

turned to Harry and said, "I didn't know whether I wanted to meet you at all, I have heard many things about you." Surprised, he responded, "Your Majesty, I am not half so bad as I look, nor one-quarter so bad as you seem to think I am." She smiled and said that the King had told her that he wasn't exactly a heathen, so she had decided really to form his acquaintance. They spent a very pleasant time at the breakfast table, in which considerable repartee was indulged in, despite the Royal presences.

From breakfast until they were able to leave later in the afternoon, Harry was subjected to a royal diatribe on how poorly the Romanians were being treated, and how they felt they had every reason to loot Hungary to their pleasure. In the Queen's own words, "You may call it stealing if you want to, or any other name, I feel that we are perfectly entitled to do what we want to." She seemed to have conveniently forgotten her thoughts of an earlier time. When Romania was over-run by troops of the German-Austro-Hungarian armies, during the war in 1916, the King and Queen were forced to abandon their home and go into exile. When she was able to return to her residence, after a two-year absence, she is quoted, "In all fairness to the overthrown, I would mention that whatever loot or destruction they gave way to in other houses, our invaders behaved well whilst in possession of our personal habitations, and we found but little missing on our return."[136]

The King added that at least the Romania troops did not take food from the Hungarians. Harry responded by stating that he had incontrovertible proof that thousands of carloads of food items had been taken out of Budapest alone.

Prior to taking his leave, the Queen presented Harry with a photo portrait of herself, autographed it, and told the General that she hoped that whenever he felt ill about the Romanians

---

[136] *The Country that I Love*, by Marie, Queen of Roumania

he should look at it as a reminder of their good visit.[137] This very vain woman shared Harry's thoughts on her beauty. She is quoted as stating, "I am said to be the most beautiful woman in Europe. About that, of course, I cannot judge because I cannot know. But about the other queens, I know I am the most beautiful queen in Europe."[138]

Four days later, King Ferdinand signed Royal Decree 4181, bestowing upon General Bandholtz, the Order of the Romanian Crown, with sword, and the rank of Grand Cross.[139] According to the U.S. Army Adjutant General's Records there was only one honor of this class given to an American.

---

[137] *The photo of Queen Marie remained in the Bandholtz home long after his death.*
[138] *The Last Romantic The Life of the Legendary Marie, Queen of Roumania," Hannah Pakula, Simon and Shuster*
[139] *Bandholtz awards and citations, US Army Military Police Museum, Ft Leonard Wood, MO*

## Chapter Seventeen

## PRESSURE THE OCCUPIERS

After his visit with the Romanian Royal Family, Harry returned to Budapest and went back to work. It was not long before the four allied generals wrote to the Peace Commission, in Paris, that the Romanians were hindering every effort to arm the police of Hungary, and the formation of Hungarian Defense Forces. After promising 4,000 pistols, they reneged and stated the Hungarians would have to find their own sources of weaponry.[140]

A short time later another British Officer, serving as an observer, reported that he had seen the following crossing a bridge over the Theiss River, heading for Romania: "684 locomotives, 231 saloon and private cars, 946 passenger coaches, 2,900 empty box and flat cars, 1,300 mixed carloads of grain, cattle, etc., 1,300 carloads of munitions, 298 cannon, three autos, 56 aeroplanes (sic), 1,400 oil tanks, 2,000 carloads of railway material and agricultural machinery, 1,435 of war material, 4,350 contents not visible; also many miscellaneous cars, making a total of 17,319 locomotives and cars." No matter what the allies wanted, the Romanians were determined to get away with as much as possible. In his diary for September 17, Harry writes: "I then submitted to the Mission the Hungarian financial question, which is getting into acute stages, and which shows that our Roumanian (sic) allies have business ideas which would do credit to the Buccaneer Morgan." The situation was not all bad, as the British Observer also noted that troop-trains, with Romanian soldiers were seen heading home. The Red Cross had also been contacting the Allied Mission regarding the poor treatment of Hungarian Prisoners of War being held by the Romanians.

---

[140] *Mission Reports, Bandholtz Papers, Hungarian National Museum*

On September 19, General Bandholtz had been informed of Austrian, and other European newspaper accounts of atrocities committed against Jews, some were reported as perpetrated by Hungarian White Army forces. On the 29$^{th}$, Colonel Nathan Horowitz, a Jew himself and member of Bandholtz's staff, reported after his tour of Hungary, that Admiral Horthy's Army had done everything within reason to prevent any such mistreatment of anyone. This was reported to the Peace Commission in Paris, with a request that the correct information be provided to the newspapers concerned.

Admiral Horthy, the commander of Hungary's new Army, organized a counter-revolution against the communist government of Bela Kun. Under Kun, there were daily murders and unjustified prosecutions. Because Kun and several of his followers were Jews, a Hungarian backlash against Jews was feared. In retrospect Anti-Semitism had never been a trait of the Hungarian people or it's government. His army became known as the White Army, to differentiate it from Bela Kun's communist forces.

Into October the problems persisted, and pilfering treasures from Hungary's museums was being reported. It was the opinion of the Romanians that since they were to be given part of Hungary's territorial lands, they were entitled to a percentage of the items in their museums. They were ordered by the Mission to discontinue the removal of any articles.

However, on Saturday, the 5$^{th}$ of October, Romanian authorities reported that the first phase of withdrawing their forces had been accomplished without incident. Both British and American observers verified this. Feeling a sense of relief, Harry went to his quarters for an evening of relaxation. However, it was on that very same evening when a report was received about Romanian Army Troops, being at the door of the Hungarian National Museum, in downtown Budapest. This building holds the nation's most important treasures and the soldiers were making demands of the director to allow them access to the interior.

The General heard this news, from Colonel Horowitz as he was finishing his evening meal, around 9:30 PM. He called for Colonel Loree, along with an enlisted driver, and followed Horowitz to the museum. Not in the mood for putting up with more looting, he instructed the driver to speedily get to the museum. Going down the winding cobble-stone road, from Buda Castle, they crossed over the Széchenyi lánchíd, or Chain Bridge, and on to Jozsef Attila Street, right on Karoly, and right again onto Muzeum Krt. Pulling into the circular drive of the museum, they were confronted by a group of Romanian soldiers, numbering around 40, with a dozen or so trucks. The Romanian soldiers tried to stop him, but he brushed them aside, ignoring their protests. He stormed into the museum, where he found the museum's director, embroiled in a discussion with the Romanian Commander. The Romanian was demanding the keys, stating that if he were not allowed to enter the exhibits, he would storm the museum the following morning.

Hungarian National Museum, photo by author

General Bandholtz asked, "What in Hell do you think you are doing?" Brandishing his riding crop, he told the Romanian officer that the property within the museum was under the jurisdiction of the Inter-Allied Commission, he was President of the Day, and ordered the man to remove himself and his troops. The Romanian Commander tried to explain that he was under orders from Commissioner Diamandi and General Mardarescu to retrieve all articles within the museum, which had come from Transylvania. Bandholtz repeated his order that the Romanians leave the museum property, taking their trucks with them. He then received the keys to the museum from the Director, and left him a handwritten order, which read, ""To whom it may concern – As the Inter-Allied Commission is in charge of all the objects within the Hungarian National Museum, at Budapest, the key has been taken charge of by the President of the Day, General Bandholtz, the American Representative." He then locked all the doors. Signs were posted on each of the doors, which read: "This door sealed by Order the Inter-Allied Military Commission. H. H. Bandholtz, President of the Day, October 5$^{th}$, 1919." He added in his diary the following day, "As the Romanians and all Europeans are fond of rubber-stamp display, and as we had nothing else, we used an American mail-censor stamp, with which we marked each of the seals."

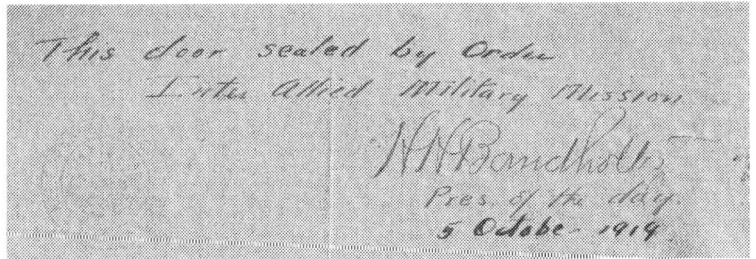

One of three seals placed on doors,
with permission Hungarian National Museum

Two days after the museum incident, the Romanian Commander of Budapest, General Mosoiu, the successor of General Holban, invited General Bandholtz and his entire staff to lunch. Harry described it as a "Love Fest," with an honor guard and band at the entrance to the Hotel Hungaria. The band played a poor rendition of "The Star Spangled

Banner," and repeated this piece while inside the banquet facilities. All seemed as though nothing had occurred and that the allies were all in accord.

The month of October passed with more reports of looting, by the Romanians, but not at the museum, maltreatment of prisoners of war, and the removal of funds from various banks. A study group, including medical doctors, was ordered to inspect all detention facilities where the Romanians were holding Hungarian troops. Ten thousand rifles were offered to arm the Hungarian Police but none actually arrived.

The study group was formed to look into the Prisoner of War Issue. The results of their examination were reported to the Romanian Army. Conditions in the camps were disgraceful, and that reflected on the Allies. The Mission directed that eight steps be taken to improve conditions in the camps, which were basically simple hygiene and humanitarianism.

IAMM and Romanian Generals watch Romanian troops in review

The Romanian Army began evacuating Budapest on November 13$^{th}$, and almost immediately, reports started coming in of troops pilfering houses and farms on their way out. Romanian commanders were contacted and told, in no uncertain terms, that the looting was to stop. In a seemingly grandiose gesture, the Romanians stated they were going to distribute large quantities of foodstuffs, to the suffering Hungarian populace. This welcome news was received with glee, until it was learned the distributed food was coming from Hungary's own warehouses, causing a problem with Hungary's own rationing program.

It was during this period, that a representative of the American Red Cross began a child-feeding program, by feeding upwards of 100,000 children per day. During an eight month period, beginning in January 1920, The American Relief Action for Hungary distributed another 189,116 pounds of cocoa; 737,440 of sugar; 545,377 boxes of condensed milk; 1,193,524 pounds of flour; 497,453 of rice; 102,414 of lard; 35,952 of oil; 62,982 tins of fish. This was in addition to 50,000 pairs of shoes and boots; 500,000 stockings; 19,700 overcoats; 17,000 boys' suits and 13,940 girls' frocks.[141]

On the 16th of November, the Hungarian White Army, under the command of Admiral Milklos Horthy, took over the occupation of Budapest.

Admiral Horthy enters Budapest,
with permission Hungarian National Museum

---

[141] *American Hungarian Relations 1918-1944*, by Mark Imre Major, Danubia Press, 1974

Horthy had been appointed Commander-in-Chief of all Hungarian Armed Forces during 1919, and led his National Army into Budapest upon the evacuation of the Romanian forces. Shortly after his arrival he proclaimed to the leadership and assembled citizens: "Mr. Mayor! In the name of the Hungarian National Army, I offer you my sincere thanks for your warm words of welcome. Today, on the threshold of this city, I am not prepared to speak in conventional phrases. My sense of justice compels me to tell you what is uppermost in my mind at this moment. When we were still far distant, when our hope of returning to this poor, ill-fated city, arms in hand, was the merest glimmer, we cursed and hated her, for from afar we saw only the mire into which she had sunk and not the persecution and martyrdom which our Hungarian brethren were suffering." He added, "this city has disowned her thousand years of tradition, she has dragged the Holy Crown and the national colors in the dust, she has clothed herself in red rags. The finest of the nation she threw into dungeons and drove into exile. She laid in ruin our property and wasted our wealth." Further he stated, "We shall forgive this misguided city if she will turn from her false gods to the service of her fatherland, if with all her heart and soul and strength she will return to her love of our land in which the ashes of our ancestors rest and which our brethren till with the sweat of their brows, if she will revere once more the Holy Crown, the Double Cross, the Three Hills and the Four Rivers, in short, our Hungarian fatherland and our Hungarian people. My soldiers, after they had gathered in the harvest, took up arms to restore order in the Fatherland. Now their hands are held out unencumbered to you in friendly greeting, but these hands remain ready to mete out punishment and to strike blows should the need arise. We extend to our fellow sufferers, who have endured so much tribulation and who yet gave us their sympathy, our heartfelt salutation."[142] With the arrival of Admiral Horthy's

---

[142] *The Annotated Memoirs of Admiral Milklos Horthy, Regent of Hungary, Simon Publications, 1957*

Army, the changes over-all were very favorable. The soldiers were well disciplined as they began their duties.

On the 17th, Generals Bandholtz and Gorton met General Mardarescu before he left Budapest. The Romanian General promised faithfully to leave behind fifty-three motor trucks for the distribution of food. When men went to get the trucks, instead of fifty-three they found only thirty-six, not one of which was serviceable and most of which were lacking in wheels, motors, or something equally important, but when Mardarescu left, he even took these along.

Sir George Clerk, Allied Commissioner to Romania, in evident fear that he was not going be able to accomplish his mission, sent some telegrams to Paris, which apparently gave the impression that Admiral Horthy and Minister Friedrich[143] were arresting all of their political opponents. Harry noted in his diary, "As a matter fact, the arrests that were made were practically insignificant, and none were made that were not perfectly justifiable. Under the circumstances, I was obliged to telegraph the American Commission accordingly."

Meeting to discuss feeding of Budapest's Children
with permission Hungarian National Museum

---

[143] István Friedrich (July 1, 1883 - 1951) was a Hungarian politician who served as prime minister of Hungary for three months in 1919, and remained Minister of Defence until March 15, 1920.

At a meeting with the new Hungarian Prime Minister, on the 30th of November, Harry was asked if the riding crop he was carrying was the same one he carried while turning the Romanians away from the National Museum. After responding affirmatively, the Prime Minister asked that Harry donate it to the museum, to be kept with the "seals" he had placed on the doors. Harry reluctantly turned over the crop, which he was very fond of. (The riding crop remains on display, in the Museum, to this day!)

On December 3, 1919, General Bandholtz sent a memo, to the Hungarian General Staff, entitled "Notes on a public meeting which took place on November 30, 1919," regarding the treatment of Jews. In the document he quotes various speakers to the meeting. The first paragraph quoted, a Catholic Priest, Demetrei Kovary, "The Bible tells us that we must forgive our enemies. I say we can personally forgive our enemies as Christians, but not as Hungarians. The Hungarian people must never forget these things, the Jews must be punished." Kovary preceded these remarks by an opinion that Jews were the cause of the general demoralization of Hungary. They had corrupted the morals and the religion of the people, had worked through the press and their propaganda, and laughed at Christianity, trying every way to destroy Christian religions.[144]

Another speaker, an officer of the Hungarian White Army, stated he represented thirty-six Christian Societies, which were ready to stand by their brothers in Budapest. He added that in the section from which he came, the Jews were so bad that they sold their wives and daughters and have altogether too many rights which must be taken away." [145]

These words reflect the general mistrust of Jews, who were thought of as being responsible for the introduction of communism to Hungary. It was from them that Bela Kun had gotten most of his support.

---

[144] *Untitled Memo, Hungarian Military Archives*
[145] *Ibid*

Later in the month of December, Harry was notified by the US State Department that a Civil Commission, designed to assist the Hungarians in the formulation of their new government, was replacing him. He was relieved of duty with the Commission, but ordered to remain in Budapest as the American Military Representative to Hungary.

## Chapter Eighteen

# THE ROMANIAN PERSPECTIVE

So much criticism had been directed at the Romanians from all quarters, that the Romanian Government, in 1919, invited an American academic, Charles Upson Clark, to observe first hand the situation on the ground. Dr. Clark had been a member of the American Academy in Rome from the turn of the century and had written other histories. While he readily admits his Romanian bias, he also states he tried to be accurate and fair.

The results of his studies, during 1919-1927, were written in the book, "Greater Roumania,"[146] published in 1922. A second version, "United Roumania," was launched in 1932. The latter version updated some material, and deleted some chapters, notably that dealing with an audience with King Ferdinand and Queen Marie.

In his treatment of the World War era, Clark elaborated on the Treaty of Bucharest of 1916, when Romania agreed to enter the war on the side of the Allies, while Russia, England, Italy and France guaranteed the territorial integrity of Romania and promised to provide the latter with the arms and ammunition to conduct war. The Allies also agreed to award Romania the disputed lands of Transylvania, and other lands then held by Austria-Hungary. The boundaries of the lands to be annexed, upon a successful completion of the war, were outlined in the treaty. Other sources state Queen Marie demanded the annexation provision, before she would encourage King Ferdinand to enter the war on the Allied side.

---

[146] *Greater Romania, by Charles Upson Clark, Dodd, Mead and Company, 1922*

To prepare for war, Romania mobilized 850,000 men, but had only 440,000 rifles for them. Of these 330,000 were modern, German manufactured Mannlicher Rifles, while the remainder was older single shot types, or war relics captured from Bulgaria in 1913. The 1916 Treaty called for the Allies to supply war materials, at the rate of 300 tons daily. Romania had only 500 machineguns, little artillery, no modern aircraft, a few vehicles and was lacking in communications equipment, gas masks, anti-aircraft guns, and basic necessities. While some supplies were arriving, Romania always felt the allies were not upholding their part of the bargain. Most were far removed, geographically; so all supplies were to come through Russia. Turkey, one of the Central Powers, had closed the Dardanelles, thereby restricting access to the Black Sea, and Romania's ports, from the Mediterranean. As a result, Romania was isolated from all of her Allies, except for Russia, just across the Black Sea.

The Romanian and Russian armies fought few severe battles with the Germans, had some successes, but also lost territory. In 1917, Russia negotiated an armistice with Germany, which left Romania as an isolated state. Rather than annihilation, she chose an armistice with Germany, signing the Treaty of Bucharest in early 1918. As a result, German armies occupied Romania and inflicted serious financial distress, through confiscations, reparations, and outright theft. Romania was required to demobilize the majority of her army. Most of her food supplies and production were used to feed and clothe the Germans.

The tide changed against Germany during 1918, when the World War ended in November of that year. War's end, however, did not bring peace. Many countries were in disarray, and governments were changing. Bela Kun led his communist party to power in Hungary and his Red Army attacked both Serb and Romanian positions, to force them from occupied lands. This weak foray was repulsed and Bela Kun withdrew his forces to regroup. In July, he again attacked on two fronts and was once again defeated. The road to Budapest was now open. Romania managed to rout Bela Kun's forces and her troops marched to Budapest. Czech forces also occupied portions of its border with Hungary.

Clark's research told him that Romania, instead of being a pariah in Budapest, was more like a savior. He states that Romania brought law and order, while the Inter-Allied Military Commission said quite the opposite. To counter Allied claims that Romanian troops were depriving Hungarian school children of food and milk, Clark attributed the milk shortage to hoof and mouth disease in Hungarian dairy herds. In responding to allegations of misuse of prisoners of war, held by the Romanians, he stated that their own lack of food and blankets were responsible for the poor conditions.

As for the general looting and taking of hospital supplies, Clark followed the line of King Ferdinand and Queen Marie that Romania was entitled to take whatever they wished, because it was theirs to begin with. His book contained photographs of supplies, allegedly stored in Budapest hospitals, bearing Romanian writings and shipping documents or labels.

Going still further, the attempt to sack the Hungarian National Museum was described as an effort to remove only those artifacts which pertained to Transylvania, or other areas, which were promised to Romania at the Treaty of Bucharest in 1916.

About the promises made by Romania officials, that were never fulfilled, Clark mentions little. For example, after several promises to provide arms for a Hungarian police force, these never materialized. Vehicles provided for the distribution of food, to those in extreme distress, were stripped of their major components and left virtually worthless.

On February 21, 1920, the New York Times published a letter, to their editor, from a C. Cihodariu, rebutting General Bandholtz's charges. This was under the heading *"Rumanians in Hungary, A Defense Against the Charges of General Bandholtz."* Basically, this letter states that Romania was defending herself against Hungarian attack, and occupied Budapest and other territories as a means to safeguard her own borders. This was followed by another letter, to the same newspaper, described as, *"Hungarian Complaints,"* printed in the June 28$^{th}$, 1920 Edition. In this latter letter, the author, a Mr. Joseph S. Sugar, contradicts Mr. Cihodariu, and offers proof of the allegations made by General Bandholtz and other officials. Whatever the truth may be, it probably lies somewhere between the vast differences between the Romanian and Allied versions of the tale. There is no doubt; the Allies had not supported Romania, as promised in the earlier treaty of 1916. However, with the Russian-German Armistice,[147] the lines of supply were lost. Romania also lost favor when she signed a separate peace treaty with Germany,[148] months before November, when the war officially ended. There exists many reports of compassionate treatment, by Romanian soldiers, of Hungarian prisoners and wounded during the war.

---

[147] *Russo-German Armistice, between Bolshevik Russia and Germany, 16 December 1917*
[148] *Romania surrendered to the Central Powers on May 7, 1918. However, the resulting Treaty of Bucharest never completed ratification in Romania and was denounced in October 1918 by the Romanian government, which then re-entered the war on the Allied side*

## Chapter Nineteen
## THE SERBS

In the same time frame as Harry received his notification, that he would soon be relieved by a Civil Commission, the Serbs seemed to take over where the Romanians had left off. They refused to withdraw from occupied territories. This however, did not affect the City of Budapest but was located in more rural areas, especially in the vicinity of Pécs, a large mining area, of Hungary.

The Serbs complained to the Commission that the Hungarian Army had invaded their troops with one thousand troops crossing the Serbian Line, in an attack. They were demanding release of all prisoners and reparations. After contacting, and being briefed by the Hungarians, it was learned there were no regular Hungarian troops in the area, only a company of gendarmes (policemen). These gendarmes were conducting an operation in the vicinity of Serbian lines, and the Serbs thinking they were being attacked, the latter came out of their lines to surrender."

The Inter-Allied Military Mission kept receiving reports, regarding Serbian troops looting in the vicinity of Pecs. A Serbian Minister was brought before the Commission, and asked to explain his government's actions. The Minister stated he had read newspaper accounts of these incidents of thievery and had so notified his government in Belgrade. They replied that he was to deny this as being without foundation. General Bandholtz then took the floor, and said, "My Dear Doctor, why in Hell do you insist on imitating the Romanians in everything. We know that your people are requisitioning and seizing property around Pecs; you know that they are doing it; and the proofs are right here before you. Now why imitate and blindly follow Romanian tactics, and try to lie out of it under all these circumstances?" In return, the minister acknowledged the wrongdoing of Serbian soldiers and promised to look further into the matter.

While this seemed to satisfy the immediate circumstances, the Serbian Government was still angry over the alleged incident of their being attacked. The Serbian Parliament had ordered all food shipments into Hungary halted. It fell upon a Canadian Captain, a member of the British Food Committee, to negotiate a way to resolve the food problem, while the Hungarian populace was in dire straits. The Serbs agreed to lift the embargo providing the Hungarians apologized for the incident. Hungary was to release all Serbian prisoners; pay reparations to the families of any Serb injured during the incident, in accordance with fees established by the Inter-Allied Commission, and give assurances that no further incidents would take place. The Commission, in turn, requested that Admiral Horthy, the Hungarian Premier, follow these instructions through normal diplomatic channels. The following day, General Bandholtz again spoke to the Serbian Minister, and with a little arm twisting, got the Minister to immediately telegraph the government in Belgrade to release 5,000 carloads of food, which were being delayed, also the Hungarians had already made payment. After concluding this business, the general went to the Hungarian offices to insist that they take immediate action in getting the apologies sent to the Serbs. This was done within the next few days.

Notified by telegram, from the State Department, that a civil Commissioner, Mr. U. S. Grant-Smith, was leaving the United States to take over his duties, Harry notified his counter-parts on the Mission, by letter to each. The blanket letter stated: "My dear General: It is with a feeling of real regret that I am obliged this date, as per my official communication to the Inter-Allied Military Mission, to sever for myself the close and harmonious official relations that have from the beginning existed between me and my colleagues of the Inter-Allied Mission. My association for four months with three generals of international fame has been for me a great honor, a privilege and an education. Your patience under the steady fire of my Americanisms has been admirable but has also been appreciated. I shall ever retain most pleasant and affectionate recollections of each and all of you. Signed, H. H. Bandholtz, Brig. Gen., U.S.A."

He also wrote to the Prime Minister of Hungary, December 13, 1919, "I have the honor to inform your Excellency that on this date, pursuant to instructions from the American Commission to Negotiate Peace, I shall cease to be a member of the Inter-Allied Military Mission, but shall remain temporarily in Hungary as American Military Representative. H. H. Bandholtz, Brig. Gen., U.S.A."

With his fifty-fifth birthday approaching on December 18, Harry organized a birthday celebration at the offices of the American Mission. Somehow his invitations failed to include the Archduke Joseph of Hungary, and Archduchess Augusta, formerly Augusta Maria Louise Princess of Bavaria (1875-1964), although their son and daughter had been invited. In his diary is written, "Yesterday afternoon the young Archduke [whom he often referred to as the Dukelet] called up a friend of mine and said that he was in a Hell of a fix, or words to that effect, that he and his sister had been invited to General Bandholtz's birthday party but that Papa Archduke and Mama Archduchess had not been included, that papa and mama were crazy to come, but were a little bit afraid of General Bandholtz and did not know how he could be approached, and would my friend be so kind as to try to arrange the matter." Harry went that very afternoon to extend a personal invitation to the Archduke and his wife, and recorded, "Archie" was tickled to death, and showed it, and he sure would be there with the entire Archducal family.

On the 17th, Budapest's largest newspaper, the "Pester Lloyd" printed the following tribute: *"Harry Hill Bandholtz: Tomorrow, the eighteenth of December, is the birthday of Brig. Gen. Harry Hill Bandholtz, U.S.A., the leader of the American Military Mission to Hungary, who won fame in the*

*Philippine War. It is not essential for us to know where he was born and what age he will be tomorrow, as we respect in this son of the great Union only the noble, energetic, kind-hearted, and strong man, who combines the virtues of the old soldier with the qualities of a most capable diplomat. Yes, we love and honor General Bandholtz, who visited Budapest as the first representative of the United States, thus awakening within us those sympathies which we have ever harbored since the beginning of the war, for the nation of George Washington, Abraham Lincoln and Thomas Jefferson. He has since done everything to increase this enthusiasm and sympathy. We owe this noble man a great debt of gratitude for his work of mediation, which he is doing for us in all quietude, but none the less energetically in our much-tried country. We avail ourselves of this opportunity to express to him the warmest wishes of every Hungarian and trust that he may live see many a happy return of this day, in good health and good spirits."*

The party called for a dance after dinner, and The Archduchess Augusta requested that they dance a Hungarian "Csardas," which General Bandholtz described in his diary. "In this dance, you face your partner squarely, the lady puts both arms upon your shoulders and looks soulfully into your eyes, you place both hands on her hips and ditto the soulful stunt. You then wiggle back and forth to the right and left with a couple of side jumps, occasionally intermingled with a hundred-yard dash speed on a ring-around-the-rosy with your partner." Watching the dancing, Harry got a basic understanding of the maneuvers, and was ready when approached to dance, by the Countess Teleki, wife of Pál Count Teleki de Szék, Foreign Minister of Hungary. "We took a catch-as-catch can hold and then showed the Archduke and assembled multitude how the "Csardas" should be danced." The Archduke applauded vigorously and General Gorton nearly cracked his monocle by his rapid change of facial contortions. The Archduchess had intimated in the beginning that she wanted to be treated in a strictly

American manner and she surely got it. The party did not break up until after 5:30 AM, of the 19th.

Having received many birthday gifts from his guests, one letter of acknowledgement deserves special mention. His British colleague, General Gorton, from the Inter-Allied Military Mission, presented him with a silver dish. The British General had often joked with General Bandholtz about his frequent blunt statements, during the conduct of their meetings. This seems to be an effort at doing the opposite! "My dear Gorton: In proper acknowledgement of that "pippin" of a birthday present, as scintillatingly substantial as your attractive self, I have endeavored anon and again to indite a touching epistle that would induce the weeps and melt your tinkling monocle, and which, in return for the oft-repeated and outrageous verbal assaults committed against my archducal dignity, would be as coals of fire upon your stiff and bushy pompadour. And now, in despair at doing the subject justice, I will simply say, many, many thanks and God bless you and yours, Your devoted friend, H. H. Bandholtz."

Another unexpected gift arrived after the birthday festivities. Harry received a letter from a chauffer he had while Chief of Staff of the New York Division. While he doesn't elaborate, he writes in his diary, "A courier arrived with a few letters today. Fortunately one of them was from my young friend and former chauffeur in the New York Division, Lieutenant Littwitz, who wrote me more in detail about Mrs. Bandholtz's condition than anything that I have had in months. It seems good to have somebody that can sympathize with me in my situation here and give me the kind of news that is most needed." The General and Mrs. Bandholtz had been legally separated since 1918, and she had suffered with periodic mental problems.

## Chapter Twenty

## WINDING DOWN

Rumors and reports of Hungarians murdering Jews continued. On December 22$^{nd}$, Bandholtz received news summaries from Vienna. The Arbeiter Zeitung, of the seventeenth of December, gave the Americans honorable mention, and among other things said:

"An American Commission which visited Kecskemét[149] found sixty-two corpses lying unburied or hanging on the trees of a neighboring forest. This paper is in position to prove by an official document that this wholesale murder was committed by order of the functionaries of the Hungarian state, with the knowledge of the highest authorities and of the Ministry of Justice, and that it was hushed up, though the number of victims is said to be about five thousand.

The Allied Powers are about to conclude peace with this government of murderers and thus to receive them into the community of civilized humanity. The Roumanians kept these men in check, but hardly had they left when the slaughtering began. English, French, and Americans did not permit them to protect the lives of these miserable people. The American Colonel Yates[150] undertakes the supreme control over the Brachialgewalt, that is, the new forces. Now, under the Stars and Stripes of the United States, who could hold back these monsters, the murderous work will go on."

Mr. Halstead , the American Commissioner in Austria, sent Harry the above translation and he immediately responded by telegraph as follows:

---

[149] *A Hungarian city, roughly 50 miles from Budapest*
[150] *Col. Halsey E. Yates, Chairman of the Commission on Police and Gendarmerie, serving under Gen. Bandholtz*

*Budapest, Hungary*
*Mr. Halstead, 22nd December 1919*
*Vienna.*

*B 225 Reference your Press Summary Number 81 your regrets about action of Vienna press apply particularly to article from Arbeiter Zeitung of December 17 quoted in your Press Summary Number 85. Every statement in this article as received and regarding Americans is false. No American Commission visited Kecskemét. Colonel Yates returned to his permanent duties in Roumania over three weeks ago. The American member of the Inter-Allied Military Mission was relieved from same on December 13. Report that Colonel Yates undertakes supreme control over the new forces and that murderous work is going on under the Stars and Stripes of the United States is inexpressibly false and libelous and it is requested that prompt and efficacious action be taken adequately to punish the perpetrators, to force the Arbeiter Zeitung to retract its false statements, and to prevent a repetition of such a scurrilous publication. B. 225[151]. Bandholtz."*

General Bandholtz confronted Admiral Horthy on January 20th, 1920. He described it in his diary as follows: "then I told him that I was sure it would appeal to him as being advisable to be frank with me in regard to any Bolshevist uprising, or anything of the kind; that I had repeated and almost confirmed rumors of the killing of some Bolshevists at the Ganz-Danubius Works in Budapest, and of an incipient Bolshevist uprising at Szolnok.[152] He appeared astonished at this information, and said positively that he had never heard anything of the kind; furthermore, that he had just come from Szolnok within the past twenty-four hours. He then called in his Chief of Staff, who substantiated everything that the Admiral had said. Harry recorded, "The

---

[151] *Telegram number*
[152] *A city in Central Hungary*

natural inference is that these persistent rumors of Bolshevist uprisings and killings in Hungary are due to unfriendly propaganda, but it is hard to tell just who starts it."

Admiral Horthy, wrote in his memoirs, "And the Communists in Hungary, willing disciples of the Russian Bolshevists, had indeed let hell loose. It took time for the stormy waves to subside, and for law and order once more to prevail throughout our land, in keeping with our ancient traditions. A year of revolution, of Red Terror and, as certain historians will have it, of the reprisals of the White Terror. I have no reason to gloss over deeds of injustice and atrocities committed when an iron broom alone could sweep the country clean. I considered the disbanding of units that had been spontaneously formed throughout Hungary to combat the Red Terror, and the transforming of them into well-disciplined units of the new National Army, one of my main tasks. The headquarters of this army never issued a bloodthirsty order. But I do not hesitate to endorse what Edgar von Schmidt-Pauli wrote about this period in the book he has written about me: "A troop of soldiery, hurling itself forward to create order at the risk of life, the fighting spirit and will to sacrifice having to be maintained at all costs if the leader is to achieve the great task he has set himself, cannot be reprimanded for every trifle; the officers who exceed their competence cannot always be shot or even disciplined, not, that is to say, if the danger of mutiny, or worse, is to be avoided. In times of disturbance, the military cannot be too softhearted. Hell let loose on earth cannot be subjugated by the beating of angels' wings."

Having been notified of the impending arrival, in January 1920, of the American Commissioner, Mr. U. S. Grant-Smith, Harry's duties began to wane. He spent much of his time, wrapping up loose ends, and trying to prepare for his trip home. He was invited to countless dinners, operas, shopping excursions, and sittings for a portrait. On the 22$^{nd}$, Harry was able to make telephonic contact with Mr. Grant-Smith, who had arrived in Vienna. The latter stated he would be in Budapest on the 27th, and was anxious to learn as much as possible from General Bandholtz. The General was to remain in Budapest until early February and would sail for the U.S.A., early in March. He did not relish the thought of three weeks in Paris!

Before he was to leave Budapest, Harry was able to accompany the Hungarian peace delegation, headed by Count Apponyi,[153] to Paris, arriving February 11, 1920. The Count was a noted statesman and orator, but his attendance at Paris was not well received by the Allies, and there were no negotiations to modify the agreed upon treaty. Another member of Hungary's delegation, Roland Hegedues, stated "It would be a burlesque to ask Hungary to execute these clauses (of the treaty). There is no longer means left for measuring our independence."[154]

One of the last entries in General Bandholtz's Hungarian diaries is: "While we shall all be glad to be homeward bound, yet we cannot but feel some regrets at leaving Hungary. Personally I came here rather inclined to condone or extenuate much of the Romanian procedure, but their outrageous conduct in violation of all international law, decency, and humane considerations, has made me become an advocate of the Hungarian cause. Turning over portions of Hungary with its civilized and refined population will be like turning over Texas and California to the Mexicans. The great Powers of the Allies should hang their heads in shame for what they allowed to take place in this country after an armistice."

As a result of the Treaty of Trianon, signed on June 4, 1920, the former Kingdom of Hungary lost over thirteen million of her population and more than seventy percent of land mass. Her allies, Germany and Austria were not treated nearly as badly.

---

[153] *Born Albert Apponyi de Nagyappony, on May 29, 1846, to a Hungarian Noble Family, in Vienna.*
[154] *NY Times, Feb 12, 1920*

Found in the Hungarian Bandholtz Papers[155] is the following poem, dedicated to General Bandholtz, by an unknown writer:

### A Parting Word to the American Mission

*A people far over the seas*
*Has sent its sons to us for Peace.*
*They came by ship, they came by rail,*
*Our hearts to win they did not fail.*

*They set to work right in our midst,*
*And soon found what most we missed.*
*They followed evil to the root.*
*And helped the poor and destitute*

*With helping hand and kindly word,*
*By thousand hardships not deterred.*
*They lifted up who fell to ground,*
*And saved who nearly death had found.*

*But now, my God: Of wail and woe!*
*They are commanded back to go.*
*To their great land, without return,*
*Magyars! Oh weep! Till all eyes burn.*

*Invoke on them the Blessing of the Lord,*
*May they live happy, may they make report,*
*To all our Brethren on the other shore,*
*This Nation will be thankful evermore!*

---

[155] *Bandholtz Papers, Hungarian National Museum, Budapest*

# Chapter Twenty One

## RETURN TO THE U.S.A.

General Bandholtz departed from Le Havre, France, aboard the S. S. France, on March 6th, and arrived in New York eight days later. Upon arrival in the United States, he returned to his home in Constantine. Since their separation, May Bandholtz's periods of delusion worsened. Her estranged husband continued to help her find a cure, through his support of her treatments at various hospitals and sanitariums. Her paranoia was progressive, and it was finally determined by her medical experts that she had to be committed to the State Hospital at Kalamazoo, Michigan, during June 1920. Arrangements were made by Harry to ensure that May's treatments would be continued throughout her lifetime. Her doctors expressed their opinion that May would not recover from her illness. For months following her admission, Harry received frequent letters from the hospital staff that May often had to be restrained, or confined, when her attacks on staff members would turn violent. At other times, she seemed content and a pleasure to be around, asking if she could return home.

During July Harry proceeded to Camp Funston, Kansas, where he assumed command of the 13th Infantry Brigade. Camp Funston was one of those camps formed in 1917, to quarter troops being trained for action in the World War. The Camp was formed on a portion of the Cavalry Post of Fort Riley, located near Manhattan, Kansas. Camp Funston was named in honor of a Kansan, Major General Frederick Funston, a brave soldier who saw service with the Cubans, during the Spanish American War, and again with US Forces in the Philippine Insurrection. He was awarded the Congressional Medal of Honor for service in the Philippines. More notably, however, was the importance of another brave mission.

Funston gathered a team of 90 loyal Filipinos, and disguised himself as their prisoner. Appearing as rebels, Funston and his team traveled through 100 torturous miles of dense jungle to the area near Aquinaldo's headquarters. Insurgent forces were finally encountered near their headquarters, but Funston's team produced forged documents that fooled them into thinking they were bringing their leader some valuable prisoners. When they reached Aquinaldo's headquarters, a signal was given, a brief firefight ensued, and the rebel leader was captured. Although remnants of the war continued, this struck a major blow to the cause.[156]

The 13th Infantry Brigade, Harry's new assignment, traced its lineage to December 1917, and was first assigned to the 7th Infantry Division. Formed at Chickamauga, Georgia, the unit moved to Camp Funston, sometime after the Armistice. In December 1920, the Brigade and Harry were transferred to Camp Meade, Maryland. He remained Commander of that unit until August 18, 1921, when he was appointed Commanding General, Military District of Washington.

Within this time frame, America was pouring much needed aid into the war torn countries of the "near east." Generals Leonard Wood, James Harboard, and Harry Bandholtz, were very active in supporting these efforts, by presenting their personal experiences to groups of businessmen who would be making donations. Through their efforts, the "Near East Relief Agency" was able to maintain sixty-three hospitals or clinics and supported 124 orphanages. Destitute people numbering in the millions were in need of food and other necessities of life. The land area covered by this agency stretched from Syria and Irag (Mesopotamia) in the south, through Turkey, to include the Black Sea countries of Armenia, Georgia, and what is now southern Russia. One such presentation took place in Chicago where over 1,000 businessmen heard the generals' presentations at a luncheon,

---

[156] *Hall of Fame, Kansas National Guard*

held at the La Salle Hotel, on March 15, 1921.[157] In their annual report to Congress, the Near East Relief Agency stated that over 70 million dollars had been provided, "At least 1,000,000 people are living in the Near East today who would have perished had it not been for American relief," according to the group's spokesman.[158] Harry was very active in promoting similar aid to the needy of Hungary.

The World War was shortly followed by deep financial troubles, resulting in severe deflation. Businesses continued to produce at wartime levels, but demand had fallen significantly. In other words, there was a glut of product available, but the demand had decreased, causing wholesale prices to decline by 36.8 percent.[159]

During this 1920-1921 period, there had also been unrest reported in West Virginia and other mining areas, an ongoing labor dispute between the miners and mine operators. A reported 5,000 miners armed themselves and assembled at Marmet, just south of Charleston, West Virginia. They were armed with handguns, rifles, and it was reported they also had acquired an old machinegun with 3,000 rounds of ammunition. Formed into a column, the men set off towards Logan, a distance of roughly 50 miles. On the way, new recruits joined the march until the group numbered nearly 15,000. With the approval of President Harding, the Secretary of War dispatched General Bandholtz to look into the problem, ordering the investigation of a worsening situation between striking coal miners and mine owners. Shootings had already taken place and tensions continued to build. West Virginia's Governor, Ephraim F. Morgan, had requested Federal intervention. State authorities were losing control of the situation.

---

[157] *Will Help Feed Starving, Chicago Press Tribune*, March 16, 1921
[158] *Near East Relief has Saved 1,000,000, NY Times*, July 16, 1922
[159] *The 1920-21 Deflation: The Role of Aggregate Supply*, by J. R. Vernon; *Economic Inquiry*, Vol. 29, 1991

During the early morning hours of August 26th, Harry arrived in Charleston by train and immediately met with Governor Morgan, rousing him from his bed. At 5 A.M., he contacted President Frank Keeney and Treasurer Fred Mooney, representatives of District 7, United Mine Workers Union, and ordered them to join with him at the capitol. At the meeting, Harry informed his listeners that he was not overly concerned with who was right or wrong, in the ongoing dispute, but only with the President's orders to restore law and order. He went on to state to the union representatives that he was holding them personally responsible for the march and any damages the marchers would cause. He said, "These are your people. I am going to give you a chance to save them, and if you cannot turn them back, we are going to snuff them out like that (snapping his fingers). This will never do, there are several million unemployed in this country now and this thing may assume proportions that would be difficult to handle." He also gave them a handwritten ultimatum, which was designed to satisfy those unbelievers that he meant business.[160] While this ultimatum has not been located, we are assured that the threat of military operations was contained therein if his orders were not obeyed.

Union leaders Mooney and Keeney traveled through areas where the armed miners were gathered, passing small groups until they reached a main headquarters, reading to each the ultimatum. In an area around Drawdy Creek, they met with a miner named Harvey Dillon who seemed to be in command. He questioned the union leaders and they handed him the note from General Bandholtz. There is no way Harry could have known that his handwritten ultimatum would be read by someone who served under him. Ironically, this man had served as an orderly for Colonel Bandholtz while he served in the Philippines. Dillon proclaimed, "That's his signature! I

---

[160] *The United States Army and the Return to Normalcy in Labor Dispute Interventions: The Case of the West Virginia Coal Mine Wars, 1920-1921*

served under him and would know it anywhere. Boys, we can't fight Uncle Sam, you know that as well as I do." They agreed to disband.[161]

Harry met with miners in Racine, West Virginia, and informed them of the situation. Realizing the futility of their actions, the miners began to disperse and head home. None of them wanted to take on the United States Army, as their dispute was with the mine operators.

Later that same day, Harry, heard from his long time friend from the Philippines, Major General James G. Harboard, currently serving as Deputy Chief of Staff, US Army. Bandholtz was told to prepare for infantry action against the miners and he would be given support from Army Air Forces. The famous General Billy Mitchell led the first contingent of bombers to Kanawha Field, Charleston, in preparation for operations. Additional aircraft would follow these planes, bringing the total to fourteen.

With the miners heading home, Bandholtz telegraphed Harboard that troops would not be required, he had verified the miners were standing down, boarded his train and went back to Washington.

State authorities, however, were still preparing for the worst. Not aware the miners were heading home, there were confrontations between them and the authorities. The Sheriff of Logan County, Don Chafin, had requested help from neighboring counties and the State Police. On the 28th, a gun battle erupted between striking miners and State Police, in Sharples, a mining town in Logan County. During this incident, five miners were reported killed and others wounded. Angry miners retaliated and took captive three sheriff's deputies and a Justice of the Peace of Logan County. Government Officials of West Virginia, along with three representatives of the United Mine Workers Union, left

---

[161] *The Battle of Blair Mountain*

immediately for Sharples in an attempt to calm the striking miners.

It was around midnight, when local authorities began to arrest leaders of the miners, and gunfights began again. Those miners who were awaiting transportation home rejoined the marchers, and the size of the rebellious group swelled once again. This time, however, the miners broke into company stores, stripping them of arms and ammunition, acquired some machine guns, which had been WWI war trophies, and commandeered vehicles to transport them to their positions.

Realizing that the local authorities had totally lost control of the situation, and were now a major part of the problem, General Bandholtz returned to Charleston on the $30^{th}$. It seems a "militia" of anti-union men took up positions on Blair Mountain, in Logan County. This group was opposed by a similar sized group of 10,000-15,000 miners, who took up positions at the base of the mountain. The anti-union forces skirmished with the miners, and hired private aircraft to drop homemade fragmentation bombs on the positions of the union workers. Dozens were killed or wounded during several days of skirmishing, including innocent women and children caught in the crossfire.

Elements of three infantry regiments, the $19^{th}$, $26^{th}$, and $40^{th}$, each with a machinegun company in support, had been transported to West Virginia, with more infantry being held in reserve at Camp Dix, New Jersey. An artillery company, to support the infantry, had also arrived. General Bandholtz suggested the troops stand down, but remain prepared to take immediate action.

The fourteen bombers at Kanawha Field, were fully armed, General Bandholtz ordered them on recon flights, to determine the positions of the opposing armies, but not to take action against them. The planes dropped leaflets of the President's Proclamation, to ensure that all knew the Federal Government was taking control. Using this aerial intelligence, General Bandholtz deployed his troops on September 3rd, in such a manner as to be able to crush the opposition in a pincer movement. Having his troops where he wanted, General Bandholtz ordered all belligerents to cease-fire. His terse orders were obeyed.

Although the federal troops totaled slightly over two thousand, numbers far inferior to either of the belligerent groups, the miners realized they were facing Federal troops. They began coming off the mountain without their weapons and without the red scarves used to identify them with their brother miners. Within the next couple of days, Army troops had disarmed and sent home over 5,400 miners, their weapons were found all over the mountain. Although there were continuing skirmishes, between the miners and the mine operators, there were no shots exchanged with Federal troops.

Once again, Harry had defused a volatile situation, without his forces causing any bloodshed. His firmness with the union leaders, and with the mine owners, prevented a very intense situation from becoming one of the country's great catastrophes. Every casualty had been injured or killed by the miners or representatives of the mine operators. He also refused a request from Governor Morgan to use Army troops to assist civil authorities in arresting wanted miners. After settling this affair, the General returned to his headquarters in Washington. Martial law was never declared during this potentially explosive incident, the most threatening situation the United States had experienced since the War of Rebellion.

## Chapter Twenty Two

## AMERICA'S UNKNOWN SOLDIER

At the end of World War I, many American Soldiers, Sailors and Marines failed to return home. Buried in foreign cemeteries, or battlefields, many of these were unidentified, and some simply never located. Following the European tradition, of honoring unknown soldiers, a proposal was made in the United States, during 1919, to honor one American soldier. General Peyton C. March, the Army's Chief of Staff, opposed the idea, because he felt that eventually all of America's war dead would be located and identified. However, in December of 1920, a resolution was introduced in Congress for the return, from Europe, of an unidentified American soldier to the United States, and suitably honored in a ceremony at Arlington National Cemetery. Even though the resolution passed, the argument was again raised that the Quartermaster General had identified most of the dead, and felt confident each one would be so named.

With the new administration of President Warren G. Harding, came a new Secretary of War, Newton D. Baker, who was more receptive to the idea. The date of November 11, 1921 (the third anniversary of Armistice Day[162]) was selected for the ceremony. The Army was ordered to recover the body of an unidentified soldier, from Europe, have him transported to the United States, where a funeral and burial ceremony would be conducted. Rather than simply selecting a body at random, an elaborate scheme was put into operation, designed to ensure the chosen soldier could never be positively identified. The individual must, however, have been an American soldier, and one who positively died in battle.

---

[162] *Now known as Veteran's Day*

In fact, eight unidentified bodies were selected from four different cemeteries in France. Four were exhumed and transported to mortuary services, with the remainder being designated as backup, if the original four could be identified. The four were then transported to Chalons-sur-Marne where one would be chosen. After ceremonies by French and American troops, a Sergeant Edward F. Younger, of the 50$^{th}$ US Infantry, was selected to choose the Unknown Soldier. Younger had been wounded in the war, and earned the Distinguished Service Cross for bravery.

A Frenchman, who had lost two sons in the war, provided the bouquet and the flowers would remain with the "unknown soldier," to be buried with him at Arlington. In his own words, Sergeant Younger described the selection process, "the officer of graves registration handed the roses to me. I was left alone in the chapel. There were four caskets, all unnamed and unmarked. The one that I placed the roses on was the one brought home and placed in the national shrine. I walked around the coffins three times and then, suddenly I stopped. What caused to me to stop, I don't know. It was as though something had pulled me. I placed the roses on the coffin in front of me. I can still remember the awed feeling I had, standing there all alone." The three remaining unidentified soldiers were re-interred at the Meuse-Argonne Cemetery in France.

Once selected, the remains were first afforded honors in France, and then transported to Le Havre with French and American military escort. At the port, the remains were ceremonially loaded onboard the U.S. Cruiser, U.S.S. Olympia, for transportation to Washington. As the ship left the harbor, on October 25, 1921, she received a seventeen-gun salute by the French shore batteries, and then again by French warships as the cruiser and her escort left France's territorial waters.

In Washington, responsibilities for the details of the ceremony were given to General Bandholtz, Commander,

Military District of Washington. In October, he already had his plan formulated, submitted, and it was approved. From the time the ship docked on November $9^{th}$, at Washington's Navy Yard, until the grave was closed at Arlington, he was responsible for all particulars of the honors and ceremonies. As the ship was being tied to the pier, Harry had a band playing, while the $3^{rd}$ Cavalry served as Honor Guard.

Once off the ship, the casket was taken by the Army, placed on a caisson, and escorted from the Navy Yard to the Capitol, where the "unknown soldier" was to lie in state until November $11^{th}$. Once situated within the rotunda, of the Capitol, a four-man team, representing the Army, Navy and Marine Corps, guarded the casket.

*President lays wreath, US Army Quartermaster Museum Photo*

President and Mrs. Harding were the first to visit the casket, she placing a self made silk ribbon, and he added a bouquet of red roses to the casket. Several more dignitaries added flowers and then the casket was left to the guard of honor. Public viewing was not allowed until the following day.

Until now, lying in state at the Capitol Rotunda was reserved for Presidents of the United States, members of Congress, or important military commanders. The "unknown soldier" was only the eleventh person so honored, a practice which began almost 100 years earlier, in 1824. Newspapers of the day, in describing the ceremonies, state that in excess of 90,000 citizens and dignitaries from around the world paid tribute to this soldier. Chicago readers were told, "All we know is that he was a man and a soldier, and that is enough for us." The Atlanta Constitution had the headline, "Greatest of Earth to Honor Unknown at Funeral Today."[163]

*US Army Quartermaster Museum Photo*

On November 11, 1921, three years after the war ended, America was to honor all of its war dead, by a fitting tribute to this one unidentified soldier. As the body was taken from the Capitol, and placed on the caisson for a procession to Arlington National Cemetery, a huge throng was aligned in specific order. General Bandholtz, with members of his staff, were to lead the procession, mounted on horseback. The US

---

[163] *New York Times, Chicago Tribune, Atlanta Constitution*, November 11, 1921

Army Band, and a drum corps followed them, then a composite regiment, formed with a battalion of infantry, a battalion of sailors and marines, engineer and artillery battalions, and a squadron of cavalry. These troops were all stationed in the immediate area of the nation's capital. Next followed four military chaplains, two active and two retired. The horse-drawn caisson carrying the casket followed the chaplains. Aligned on both sides of the caisson were a group, comprised of members of all services, eight non-commissioned officers, and twelve generals and admirals. The enlisted men walked closest to the casket, and the flag officers walked as an outer file. Each of the flag officers had served during the War.

Following the caisson, President Warren G. Harding marched with General Pershing to his left, followed by Vice President Calvin Coolidge and Chief of Naval Operations, Admiral Robert Coontz. Then came the Chief Justice of the Supreme Court, William H. Taft, and Commandant of the Coast Guard, Rear Admiral William F. Reynolds, the remainder of the Supreme Court Justices followed by members of the President's cabinet, state governors, and members of Congress

A section of the Army Drum Corps followed the Congressmen, and then marched recipients of the Medal of Honor. All living holders of the medal had been invited, but only those from the World War were provided transportation at government expense. They marched eight abreast, and in order of the date of their award. Former President Woodrow Wilson in a carriage; physically unable to march followed the Medal of Honor holders. Also included in the procession were representatives from each of the state governments, veteran's organizations, fraternal groups, and welfare and patriotic societies.

Once the body left the Capitol, at 8 A.M., an artillery battery fired a single gun every minute, pausing only at noon for the two-minute period of silence, until all ceremonies had been completed. The parade followed a route past the White House, where the President and a number of dignitaries left the procession, to travel the remainder by car. Those on foot, continued to Arlington, where the casket was placed into an amphitheater near the tomb. Ceremonies began when President Harding arrived, just before noon. The Marine Band played the National Anthem; the Army Chief of Chaplains presented an invocation, and a bugler sounded attention. It was then that the two-minute period of silence took place.

Once the artillery battery continued with firing of one round per minute, the assembly, accompanied by the Marine Band, sang "America." The President followed with a tribute to the Unknown Soldier, and a plea for an end to all wars. After a hymn by a quartet from New York's Metropolitan Opera Company, President Harding placed a Medal of Honor, and a Distinguished Service Cross on the casket. He was followed by a series of foreign representatives who laid awards from their nations on the casket. This was followed by scripture readings, and in conclusion, the congregation sang the hymn, "Nearer My God To Thee."

The Marine Band left the Amphitheater and proceeded to the burial location. Here they played, "Our Honored Dead," as the casket, led by the clergy, was moved to the tomb. Again the body bearers and honorary pallbearers escorted the casket this final short distance. The burial service was read, a wreath was placed at the tomb, and Crow Indian Tribal Chief Plenty Coups, representing all Indians who had served, placed his war bonnet and coup stick at the tomb. As the casket was being lowered, the artillery battery fired three salvos, and a lone bugler played "Taps." As the last note sounded, the battery fired a final twenty-one gun salute.[164]

It was reported that no King or potentate had ever been accorded such a tribute in the history of mankind. It was a

---

[164] *The Last Salute: Civil and Military Funeral, 1921-1969*

fitting ceremony, not so much to the individual entombed that day, but symbolically to all those men who served their country during troubled times. It certainly shows the utmost respect that General Bandholtz held for his fellow military comrades.

After the burial, the Nation's Capitol returned to its routine. The nation was at peace and people were enjoying the various forms of recreation. Later that month Harry made a short trip, traveling to Constantine, where he filed a ten-page Bill of Complaint, on November 21$^{st}$, 1921, in the Circuit Court for the County of St Joseph, against May C. Bandholtz, asking that their marriage be dissolved. In this bill, he outlines the problems occurring between he and May during their thirty years of marriage.

## Chapter Twenty Three

## THE KNICKERBOCKER SNOWSTORM

Back at Fort Meade, it was not long before disaster struck Washington and General Bandholtz's expertise was needed once again. During the evening of January 28th, 1922, hundreds of people funneled into the Knickerbocker Cinema, at 18th Street and Columbia Road. This 1,700-seat theater was the most modern, lavishly decorated theater in the city. It was truly an opulent setting for an evening of entertainment. The building included three levels, was of red brick construction, with a limestone façade.

The evening program featured a film, "Get Rich Quick Wallingford," a movie about shady business dealings. It had been released only a month earlier starring veteran actors Sam Hardy and Norman Kerry. An estimated three hundred people had braved the weather and were in attendance. Snow had started falling the previous day and before the evening show, the snow had reached an accumulation of over two feet.

During intermission, at around 9 PM, the orchestra was playing as the moviegoers returned to their seats. The accumulated wet snow on the roof was heavier than the building could handle. At first, a crack appeared in the ceiling, a loud noise was heard, and the roof collapsed into the theater. Within seconds, the building was in shambles. The falling ceiling caused the occupied balcony to give way, and sections of brick wall were pulled inward. Dozens of people were trapped under the falling debris. Loss of electricity caused the theater to go dark, and only the moans and cries of the injured could be heard.

Calls for help went out immediately, the response was quick. Two Navy nurses, who happened to be in the vicinity, were able to immediately provide first aid, remaining until other medical assistance began arriving. Another passerby spent four hours extricating trapped survivors from the wrecked building. This man would go on to gain fame as U. S. Navy Admiral Richard B. Byrd, the first man to visit the South Pole, [165]

Harry ordered local troops to assist in rescue operations. Within just a few hours hundreds of soldiers were helping with rescue operations. Among them was Captain C. W. Hoover, of the Quartermaster Corps, with a 5-truck convoy, traveling the hazardous streets to reach the scene of this human catastrophe. Over the course of the next 36 hours he and his men were pulling the dead and seriously injured victims from the twisted wreckage, and were credited with saving many lives. At the scene of the tragedy, people were going through the rubble screaming for loved ones, and trying to assist the injured that could be located. First responders worked together trying to remove the masses of timber, bricks and concrete, which now covered the lower level of the building.

Disaster Scene, US Gov't Photo

---

[165] *The Admirable Admiral-Richard E. Byrd, Masonic Americana 1976*, by Warren H, Deck, pgs 201-203

Soldiers, policemen and firemen, had cordoned off the area and were working feverishly to rescue the injured. Heavy equipment was ordered and began to arrive. By 2 AM, many hundreds of additional rescuers were on the scene. They removed layers of roofing material, to expose the balcony area, lifted out concrete slab remnants of the balcony to get to the bottom level, where the majority of people had been seated.

Rescue operations continued into mid afternoon of the next day. Area hospitals were overwhelmed with the victims, which totaled 98 dead and 133 seriously injured. The dead included a member of Congress. For his efficient handling of the Knickerbocker incident, General Bandholtz received a letter of commendation from the Secretary of War.

A letter dated Feb 11, 1922, [166] written by a survivor of the incident gives some insight into the tragic results. George Cole was a soldier stationed in the Washington area and the letter was written to his sister:

*Dear Ethel:*

*For your information I will tell you all I can about what happened. This is the last time I am ever going to tell anyone.*

*I was sitting in the front of the balcony all alone about four rows back. Just before the roof fell I was about to leave. There was a rumble and a loud cry and on looking up I saw the ceiling waver and then fall in a solid mass. That is, it all came down at once. Before I could grasp what was happening the balcony dropped. I had just time to drop to the floor and lie flat. The seats in front of me kept me from being pitched forward as the others in the front of the balcony were. After I fell quite a way the floor of the balcony seemed to open from under me and then I dropped through with nothing under me. The idea is that as long as I had something under me during the larger part of the drop, the force of the*

---

[166] *The letter used by permission of the grandson of George Cole, Chris Cole.*

fall on landing wouldn't be so great. When I fell through the floor of the balcony I probably didn't drop much further, but that little bit hurt me more than anything else. I then went to sleep for a while, but the screams around me woke me up. Fortunately nothing heavy fell on me, although I was practically buried under plaster and pieces of the chairs. Everything was pitch dark and as soon as I could I squirmed around and crawled out into a place that reminded me of a cave. It was almost big enough to stand in.

When the firemen arrived with flashlights they stuck them through a little opening and I could see where I was. I saw a man still conscious who asked me to get him up. He was buried as I had been, although his arm was broken. I managed to pull him out and the firemen made an opening above and hauled him through. I then saw a woman under him who also was still conscious. She begged me to stay until they could get her out. There was a big concrete block on her foot. It was too heavy for me to move and so I had to wait for a fireman to cut through and with him we managed to get her out.

I felt pretty weak myself when they lifted me through an opening in the top. They had lights all around then and I could see well. There was not a sign of a person nor of a chair, the roof covering the entire theater. I walked across the roof to the door and was taken into a house across the street where I was looked over by a doctor and had my arm bandaged. He said I needed a couple of stitches taken, but as there were more important things for the doctors to do then, he told me to have it done the first thing in the morning. After a while, I felt O.K. and borrowed an overcoat and went home. I live about a half mile up the road from the theater. The next morning I had my arm attended to and took that Monday off and went down town and bought a new overcoat.

I felt O.K. and worked up until a couple of days ago when the doctor picked the scab off my wrist and saw a little infection, so he ordered me to stay home and keep it soaked in an antiseptic. It is all right now and I expect to go back to work Monday.

My clothes were covered in blood, as I had a slight cut on my lip which bled quite a lot.

While those in the balcony had a better chance than those underneath, not a person in the first two rows of the balcony were known to have been saved. They were pitched forward and were probably killed by the fall.

I never saw the people who were sitting side of me again and believe that they too were pitched forward over the front of the balcony.

In all I don't think that I had been under there more than twenty minutes before I got out. I was one of the first ones to get out.

To illustrate how much plaster was over me, I will say that every pocket of my clothes had some in it. Even the inside pocket of my coat and my small vest pockets.

My trusty Ingersoll valued at $2.00 came through all right and is reliable as ever.

I don't know what I'll do for amusement Saturday nights as I had always attended the picture show in that particular theater, although it was not customary for me to sit in the balcony. It seems queer to me that I was in the balcony, as that was contrary to my habit.

This is about as much as I can say about it as it is a pretty hard matter to describe.

Au revoir.
George

## Chapter Twenty Four

## MILITARY RETIREMENT

During February 1922, Harry was awarded a divorce from May, and newspapers again brought up May Bandholtz's insanity, with such headlines as "Divorces Insane Wife." In a letter to the Baltimore Sun, dated February 24$^{th}$, 1922, Harry responded with the following, "Just a few days ago there appeared in the Sun and in other papers a brief notice of the fact that I had obtained a divorce from Mrs. Bandholtz, and in some cases this was under the caption, "Divorces Insane Wife." The text briefly stated that Mrs. Bandholtz had become insane on account of a report received that Harry had been lost when a German submarine sank the ship Antilles. The trouble was that the press gave out the erroneous impression while he was absent and therefore never had an opportunity to contradict it. The facts were, that when he sailed for France the first time in 1917, aboard the Antilles, it was an uneventful crossing. It was on the return trip to New York when the Antilles was sunk. He had, however, cabled Mrs. Bandholtz news of his safe arrival – this happened in September 1917. When he returned in November, the reported loss apparently had no effect on her, and she was under public observation from February 9th, 1918 until he returned to France in June of the same year. Anyone who knew May recognized that there was not slightest indication of insanity during that period. He wrote, "I do want to invite your attention to the two facts in the matter, and anyone with any legal knowledge knows that divorce cannot be obtained on the grounds of insanity – that it must be based entirely upon other occurrences prior to mental deterioration."

Two months after the divorce was finalized, Harry married Mrs. Inez Claire Gorman, a woman 25 years younger than himself. They exchanged vows on April 19, 1922, at the Hotel St. Regis, in New York City. The Reverend L. M.

Harner presided at the ceremony.[167] She was born December 5, 1889, in Maxwell, California, the daughter of John T. and Mary (Duffield) Yarborough. The marriage to Inez caused some bitter feelings between Harry and Cleveland, and Harry commented that he felt as though he had lost his only son. There had been simmering troubles between Harry and Cleveland's wife, Jean, but Harry's divorce of May, and subsequent marriage, seemed to be the breaking point.[168]

Mrs. Inez C. Bandholtz sailed from San Juan, Puerto Rico, on May 7, 1922, arriving in New York on the 11$^{th}$. The ship she traveled on was the US Army Transport "Somme." The manifest does not reflect General Bandholtz being onboard. This is interesting because after his retirement from military service, Harry was being considered for selection as Governor of Puerto Rico. Secretary of War John W. Weeks, and General Pershing were supporting this choice but President Harding was reluctant to make the appointment. With General Leonard Wood serving as Governor of the Philippines, he felt Puerto Rico should have a civilian governor.

In April of 1923, Harry began having heart problems of increased intensity, a problem that had plagued him for several years. On the 11$^{th}$ of April, while climbing a hill, Harry lost consciousness and fell. From June until September he took sick leave, resting at his quarters. His periods of faintness, and any physical activity caused shortness of breath and fatigue.

In June he received a letter from General Pershing, which alluded to promotion. In it, Pershing writes: "Referring to our conversation not long ago, regarding advancement of rank, I am pleased to advise you that the matter has been arranged according to the understanding that we had, and will come about in due time. I am delighted that you are to

---

[167] *State of NY Certificate of Marriage, #11196, dated 19 April 1922*
[168] *Biography of Major General Harry Hill Bandholtz, by Grafton H. Cook II, July 2005, unpublished*

receive this recognition and am more than sorry that your physical condition will make it impractical for you to continue in the service."

On October 28th, 1923, he reported for a physical examination at Walter Reed Army Medical Center, in Washington, D.C. The doctor's report, following the examination, stated the general had a heart problem that was moderately severe, that he was incapacitated for military service, and further that the condition was permanent.[169] He was medically retired on November 4, 1923, with the grade of Major General.

During his long years of service, Harry had amassed quite a collection of awards, citations, and letters of appreciation, along with campaign medals and awards from foreign governments. A few of these, mainly regarding his actions during the Battle of El Caney, and later during the mutinous conduct of Minnesota troops, in Augusta, Georgia, have been mentioned briefly in these pages.

On July 9, 1918, the Senate approved an act of Congress (40 Stat. L. 872) permitting members of the military forces of the United States, serving in the World War, to accept and wear certain foreign decorations. At the close of the last fiscal year, the various nations, allied or associated with the United States during the World War, awarded a total of 18,019 decorations to officers and enlisted men of the United States Army, to members of American welfare organizations and to American civilians, connected in some capacity with the allied armies or the several inter-allied commissions or who otherwise rendered meritorious services to the allied cause. The time limit prescribed in the act of Congress approved within which members of the military establishment could accept such decorations expired on July 1, 1922.

---

[169] *Physical Examination for Retirement, Oct 8, 1923, Bandholtz Papers, UMICH*

Major General Bandholtz was to receive many of these foreign honors. For Harry's service as Provost Marshal General, he received the Cross of Commander Order of the Crown, authorized by Albert[170], King of the Belgians, Harry received the Cross of Commander French Legion of Honour, which is an award given by the French Republic, for outstanding service to France. The President of the Republic is the Grand Master of the Order of the Legion of Honour. Also from France came the Commander, Croix de Guerre, with Palm. This is an award for valor to those showing heroism involving combat with an enemy force, and was most likely awarded for his service with the 58$^{th}$ Infantry, on the front.

Italy honored Harry with their Grand Officer, Order of the Crown, authorized by King Victor Emmanuel III, and Montenegro[171] presented him with two awards; Commander, Montenegrin Order of Prince Danilo (Grand Order), and the Grand Cross Montenegro Silver Medal for Valor. Nicholas,

---

[170] *Albert Léopold Clément Marie Meinrad 1875-1934 ascended the throne on the death of his uncle, Leopold II, in 1909, to reign at 16 years old. He was married on October 2, 1900 to Duchess Elisabeth Gabrielle Valérie Marie in Bavaria. At the beginning of World War I, Albert resisted the German advance and held them off long enough for Britain and France to prepare for the Battle of the Marne (6 - 9 September 1914), famously responding to the German desire to move soldiers through his country, "I rule a nation, not a road!". He served in the front lines and shared his soldiers' hardships. He led his army through the Siege of Antwerp and the Battle of the Yser and at the end of the war as commander of the Army Group Flanders, consisting of Belgian, British and French divisions, back into its own territory. He re-entered Brussels to a hero's welcome. The King declined to cooperate with the allies and maintained separate command of the Belgian forces. In 1918 Albert finally gave in to pressure and cooperated with the allies in the final offense of 1918, being made commander of the Flanders Army Group by General Foch of France. He died in a mountain climbing accident near Namur and was succeeded by his son Leopold III, who would face the Nazis in World War II. Albert's death was mourned universally.*
[171] *In World War I in 1914 Montenegro sided with Serbia against the Central Powers, suffering a full scale defeat to Austria-Hungary in early 1916. In 1918 the Allies liberated Montenegro*

King of Montenegro authorized these awards. King Ferdinand of Romania presented Harry with the Romanian Grand Cross, Order of the Crown, the only award of this class to an American.[172] Twenty-eight Americans received lesser degrees of the Romanian Order of the Crown.

With retirement papers in hand, Harry and Inez prepared to move their household to Constantine. Harry worried how his hometown neighbors would accept the new Mrs. Bandholtz. In the rural Midwest divorce was rare, and the fact that Harry was bringing home a woman much younger, would certainly raise some eyebrows. They moved into the family home, which had been used, over the years since his mother's death, to store some of Harry's accumulated collections. Once they settled in, Inez's warmth melted any feelings of animosity that may have existed.

---

[172] *Annual Report of the Secretary of War to the President, War Department Fiscal Year Ended June 30, 1923 (Washington: Government Printing Office, 1923), pages 162-174*

## Chapter Twenty Five

## THE FINAL YEARS

From his home, in Constantine, Harry wrote to General Pershing on December 20, 1923, expressing much regret that Pershing was absent at the time of his promotion and retirement. Therefore Harry was not able to thank him in person for the kind consideration received at his hands. He then added, "Secretary Weeks[173] kindly gave me a final interview in which he was most kind and subsequently sent me a letter of appreciation, a copy of which is enclosed herewith. During our interview he asked me if I would be available for any service along the lines you discussed with me and of course I replied in the affirmative."

On December 27th, the Kalamazoo Gazette, and other Michigan newspapers, reported that General Bandholtz was under consideration to be appointed Governor of Puerto Rico. The articles mentioned Secretary of War Weeks, favored Bandholtz for the position to fill the vacancy expected when the current governor resigns. The Gazette reads, "Washington, Dec 27 – Maj. Gen. Harry H. Bandholtz, retired, of Constantine, Mich., is expected to be the next governor of Porto (sic) Rico, succeeding Gov. Horace M. Towner, according to reports current here. Governor Towner will arrive in Washington within a few days and those in close touch with the situation declare he will submit his resignation to the President. His health has not been good since he resided in the tropics."[174] Regardless of all the fanfare, Horace Mann Towner remained Governor

---

[173] *John Wingate Weeks (April 11, 1860–July 12, 1926) was an American politician in the Republican Party. He served as a United States Representative for Massachusetts from 1905 to 1913, as a United States Senator from 1913 to 1919, and as Secretary of War from 1921 to 1925.*
[174] *Bandholtz Papers, UMICH*

of Puerto Rico for another six years, resigning September 29th, 1929.

During his retirement, Harry continued enjoying his extraordinary stamp collection, buying and selling, in addition to exhibiting. There was some concern, on the part of some friends, that Harry was digging too deeply into his finances to support his extravagance with stamps. It is reported he had a world ranked collection from throughout the globe, which included many unique variations.

He remained very active in promoting Aid Programs for the needy in Hungary, through Hungarian-American Social and Business Groups. Veteran's organizations and fraternal societies also took a good deal of his time. Harry was anxious to organize a museum, in Constantine, where a lot of his Philippine artifacts, old uniforms, and militaria, may be placed on display. Harry also had a very extensive library.

Caring for the flower gardens around the house gave him many hours of pleasure. Often he could be seen relaxing on the lawn furniture, when his gardening was done for the day. Heart problems persisted, however, and the University of Michigan's Hospital, confirmed the diagnosis reported earlier by the doctors at Walter Reed Army Hospital. In October 1924, he expressed his concerns in a letter to a friend, Ted Gore. In this letter he told of three separate incidents of falling over, passing out, within a period of just a few months.[175] The doctors also warned Harry that his concerns over his strained relations with Cleveland were greatly aggravating his heart condition.

May 7, 1925, a warm, bright sunny afternoon, in Constantine, Inez Bandholtz went out to join her husband, who was seated in his favorite chair, in the back yard. As she approached, she saw that he was slumped over. He had died shortly before she came out of the house. His heart had

---

[175] *Biography of Major General Harry Hill Bandholtz, by Grafton H. Cook, unpublished, July 2005*

finally given out. So ended a life, which had begun 60 years earlier, in this same small community.

Harry had previously informed Inez and several friends that he wanted no pomp at his funeral, just a simple ceremony with burial beside his parents. His desires were carried out, although many well- wishers and admirers were in attendance. The flag draped casket was laid out in the Bandholtz home, and all available seats were taken for the brief service there. The hymn, "Lead Kindly, Light"[176] was sung, followed by an invocation by the Reverend Bastian Smith, a boyhood friend of Harry.

*Lead, kindly Light, amid th'encircling gloom, lead Thou me on!*
*The night is dark, and I am far from home; lead Thou me on!*
*Keep Thou my feet; I do not ask to see*
*The distant scene; one step enough for me.*

*I was not ever thus, nor prayed that Thou shouldst lead me on;*
*I loved to choose and see my path; but now lead Thou me on!*
*I loved the garish day, and, spite of fears,*
*Pride ruled my will. Remember not past years!*

*So long Thy power hath blest me, sure it still will lead me on.*
*O'er moor and fen, o'er crag and torrent, till the night is gone,*
*And with the morn those angel faces smile, which I*
*Have loved long since, and lost awhile!*

*Meantime, along the narrow rugged path, Thyself hast trod,*
*Lead, Savior, lead me home in childlike faith, home to my God.*
*To rest forever after earthly strife*
*In the calm light of everlasting life.*

Following the service, a large funeral cortege made its way to the Constantine Cemetery, where a crowd of over a thousand had already assembled.[177] Military veterans and various organizations were represented at the graveside

---

[176] *Hymn by Fr. John Henry Newman, 1801-1890*
[177] *Great Throng At Funeral of Gen. Bandholtz, Kalamazoo Gazette, May 11, 1925*

ceremonies. The Masonic Blue Lodge, where General Bandholtz joined as a young man and advanced to a Master Mason,[178] an enthusiastic participant since his return here, furnished their funeral ritual, led by the lodge secretary. A military honor guard, of the American Legion, fired the traditional three volley rifle salute, followed by the somber bugle call, "Taps." The American Flag was removed from the casket, folded and presented to Harry's widow. The general was a member of Richard Westnedge Company No. 1, of the Spanish War Veterans, Kalamazoo, another organization represented.

After Harry's death and burial, Inez discovered they were not in the best financial shape. May's health care costs and Harry's stamp purchases were more than she anticipated. On September 14th, 1925 she applied for a "Widow's Pension," based on Harry's wartime service. She also started looking for buyers for his stamp and artifact collections. Letters were written to the Royal Hungarian Legation, among others, offering these collections for sale.

---

[178] *On 04/19/1886, Brother Harry Bandholtz became a Master Mason in the Constantine Siloam Lodge # 35 of Michigan, personal message from the Constantine Lodge Secretary.*

## Chapter Twenty Six
# THE STATUE

After the death of General Bandholtz, Hungarian-American Organizations began campaigning to honor General Bandholtz, for his activities in Hungary and for his continuing efforts on behalf of the Hungarian people. It was determined that proper recognition could be made through the erection of a statue, in Budapest, where his encounter with the Romanian soldiers took place, on the grounds of the National Museum.

Once the idea gained popularity, and necessary funding acquired, contacts were made with prominent Hungarian sculptor Miklos Ligeti.[179] Mrs. Inez C. Bandholtz provided a number of portraits and photographs of her late husband, for the project. She served as a consultant during the design phase, and must have expressed her views. A contract was agreed upon and the sculptor began his work. A variety of sources relate that the original design was thought to depict Bandholtz in a most aggressive stance with the famous riding-crop in his hand. However, no documentation substantiating these rumors has been located. The earliest known designs show a posture very similar to that on the present statue. The final design was completed, approved, and scheduled for erection in 1936.

The idea of a statue, in Budapest, honoring General Bandholtz, rankled the Romanian Government. In a strongly worded letter to the US Department of State, Romanian Minister to the United States, Charles A. Davila, stated that

---

[179] *Miklós Ligeti (1871 Pest - 1944 Budapest) was a Hungarian sculptor and artist. His sculptural style integrated elements of impressionism and realism. His major works include the statues of Anonymous (1903) erected in Budapest, Fountain of Peace, Mrs. Déry and the Cavallery Artilleryman Memorial (1937).*

his government was "greatly disturbed" by the proposal for a statue based on the actions taken by Bandholtz, and the alleged attempts of the Romanians to loot the National Museum.

Sculptor's Model
by permission, Hungarian National Museum

This protest by the Romanians caused a flurry of messages between Secretary of State Cordell Hull, US State Department and the Embassy in Budapest. At 4 PM, March 23, 1936, a telegram signed Hull, entitled "Propriety of United States Participation at the Dedication of a Statue to General Bandholtz, Former American Commander in

Hungary," was sent, addressed to Minister (Montgomery) in Hungary. This message included, "The Department is most anxious that the matter of participation by the Legation in the unveiling ceremony, which is said to be planned for July 4, be handled in such a way as to avoid giving offense either to the Hungarian or to the Rumanian (sic) Government. The Department considers that if the ceremony is being arranged as an unofficial affair you should avoid being present or represented. If, however, the Hungarian Government gives an official character to the unveiling and invites you officially to be present, you should find some excuse to be absent from Budapest and represented by a member of your staff. Any representative of the Legation should be careful not to take an active part in the ceremony, and under no circumstances should he make any remarks."[180]

One must wonder why the US State Department was fabricating stories to avoid a ceremony honoring one of its heroes. There was a group of Hungarian-American citizens raising money, along with Hungarian government officials and private citizens, who wanted to honor an American Military Officer. Harry had devoted 37 years of his life serving the United States. His assignment to Budapest, as you may recall from Chapter 16, assigned him to a branch of the State Department, for duty, "Brigadier General Harry H. Bandholtz, U. S. Army, is relieved from assignment as Provost General, A. E. F., and will report to the Assistant Secretary of State, American Commission to Negotiate Peace, Hotel Crillon, Paris, for duty." The very department he worked for was now trying devious methods to avoid appearing at a ceremony honoring the man for his service.

John F. Montgomery, Minister to Hungary, responded to the Secretary of State, by telegram, on March 27, 1936, stating, "Statue fostered by Hungarian-Americans and money raised in the United States, City of Budapest providing the site, which has not yet been selected. Statue shows General in

---

[180] *Foreign Relations, 1936, Vol 2, US Archives*

uniform holding the crop in both hands behind him and not in a defiant attitude. Ceremony will be unofficial but Regent and other high government officials will be present.

As I have been asked to speak, any excuse except compulsory absence in the United States would give offense, and I therefore propose to say that my government has instructed me to be in Washington not later than June $15^{th}$, and thus depart for my authorized leave prior to date monument could be completed and unveiled, date of unveiling not being definitely determined.

However, unconditional refusal to have legation even represented at unofficial ceremony for unveiling a statue to an American military officer of high rank will no doubt offend Hungarians and might expose us to criticism and even ridicule on the part of the Hungarian Press and public, who feel they are merely honoring a friend."

To this message, Hull responds on March 31, "The Department approves your proposal to be absent on leave in the United States at the time of the ceremony and desires to thank you for your cooperation in this respect. It is recognized that if the ceremony is attended by the Regent and other high government officials it will be necessary for the Legation to be represented, but remarks should be avoided."

Could it be that Hungary was leaning towards re-establishing her relationship with Germany? Hitler was already Chancellor, having been appointed in January 1933. Two months later he was Dictator. If Hungary wanted any chance of recovering the territories taken from her after World War I, Hitler's Germany may have been the mechanism to attain that goal.

On the other hand, Miklos Horthy, then Regent of Hungary, was not an admirer of Hitler, and wanted to keep his distance from the German leader. After refusing several invitations from Hitler, he finally did meet with him, Mussolini, and the

President of Austria, separately, all during 1936. No treaties of a military nature were signed during any of these meetings.[181]

As the situation unfolded, the dedication was pushed back and took place at 11 AM, August 23, 1936. The location was "Freedom Square," or Szabadság tér. In excess of 2,000 attended, and watched as bands played the national anthems of the United States and Hungary. Several wreaths were laid, and speeches made praising the General. Baron Zsigmond Perenyi[182] presented the principal address. He eulogized General Bandholtz as a great soldier, a fearless knight, and an upright man.[183]

Accepting the statue, on the behalf of the City of Budapest, Mayor Charles Szendy stated, "I am extremely pleased to accept this monument because it not only expresses the gratitude of Hungary, but at the same time is a model of what we Hungarians should be, upright and strong." The Commander-in-Chief of the Hungarian Army, in the name of the Regent, then laid a wreath.

The US Charge' de Affairs, James B. Stewart, also presented a wreath and remarked, "I deem it a great honor to place a wreath before this statue - a generous tribute from the Hungarian people - to a fellow countryman of mine." Mrs. Inez Claire Bandholtz an honored guest at the dedication ceremony, was given the opportunity to express her gratitude to Hungarian Officials.

Needless to say, the dedication was done in a very professional way, with no fiery speeches aimed at the Romanians or anyone else. The statue remained in place until after World War II. When the Communists took over, and Soviet Forces occupied Hungary, the statue was

---

[181] *The Annotated Memoirs of Admiral Milklós Horthy, Regent of Hungary*

[182] *Baron Zsigmond Perényi, Chairman of the Magyar Nemzeti Szövetség (Hungarian National Alliance)*

[183] *American Hungarian Relations 1918-1944*, Mark Imre Major :

removed "for repairs," and relegated to a "graveyard" of such memorials. This occurred around 1949. It was not until the 1980s, when at the request of a US Ambassador, that the statue be retrieved from the "statue graveyard," and placed in the garden of the Ambassador's residence. In 1989, when Hungary broke from behind the Iron Curtain, the statue was once again moved permanently to its original site, another dedication ceremony was organized, and the statue remains there to this day.

Author with Harry, in Budapest April 2008

## POSTSCRIPT:

1-The murder of an undercover operative of the D.C.I. is mentioned in Dexter's book (pg 182), however has not been documented through any other source. Police in Morlaiz were contacted, through a French-speaking friend, but the authorities would not acknowledge the incident or release information. Attempts to follow-up through the Information Desk, and military attaché at the US Embassy, Paris went unanswered.

2- The statement attributed to General Pershing, "Now, Bandholtz," you are going to hate me for this, "upon his appointment as Provost Marshal General, was transcribed from "The Jungle Patrol." In going through General Bandholtz' correspondence, no such message was found. His diary for 1918 has not been located.

3- Cleveland Hill Bandholtz was graduated with the Class of 1914, USMA. He served his country until his death during 1945, attaining the grade of Lieutenant Colonel. He lies at rest in Arlington National Cemetery.

4- May Cleveland Bandholtz was hospitalized several times from 1918 until 1920, for mental problems, and was institutionalized in 1921 at Kalamazoo State Hospital, Michigan, being deemed incurable. The last census showing her there was in 1930. She died in 1934.

5- Inez Claire Bandholtz died on June 1, 1974, at Three Rivers, Michigan, and is buried with her husband in Constantine Cemetery.

# APPENDIX ONE

## Draft of proposed Act of Congress creating and organizing a Military Police Corps

Be it enacted by the Senate and House of Representatives of the United States of America in Congress Assembled

Establishment. A Military Police Corps is hereby created and established as part of the Army.

Organization. The Military Police Corps shall consist of one provost marshal general with the rank of major general, of one deputy provost marshal general with rank of brigadier general, and of two colonels, eleven lieutenant colonels, twenty-five majors, fifty-three captains, forty-eight first lieutenants, eighty-four second lieutenants, and fourteen field clerks.

The enlisted force of the Military Police Corps shall consist of thirty-one sergeants major, sixteen sergeants, and of one band, two battalions and twelve additional companies.

Part of the line of Army. The band, battalions and companies provided in section two of this act and the officers serving therewith shall constitute a part of the line of the army.

Band. The military police band shall be organized as provided by law for bands of infantry regiments.

Military Police Battalions. Each battalion of military police shall consist of two sergeants major, six sergeants, eight corporals, two cooks, one mechanic, two wagoners, one buglar, sixteen privates first class, and four companies.

Military Police Company. Each company of military police shall consist of one first sergeant, one supply sergeant, one mess sergeant, one stable sergeant, twelve sergeants, twenty-one corporals, four cooks, two horseshoers, two mechanics, one saddler, two wagoners, three buglers, and one hundred and forty-nine privates first class.

Detail of Officers. Provost Marshals, Assistant Provost Marshals, battalion adjutants, and battalion supply officers, and appropriate officers to command the companies and battalions of military police shall be detailed from the Military Police Corps.

Additional Companies. The President is authorized to organize additional companies and battalions, and to increase the officer and enlisted personnel of the Military Police Corps proportionately, provided that such additions shall not increase the total strength of the Military Police Corps to exceed one per centum of the total strength of the army.

Duties. The Military Police Corps under the Provost Marshal General is charged with the apprehension of deserters absentees and stragglers from and maintenance of order among members of the army; investigation of criminal matters, pertaining to the army; custody of prisoners of war; co-operation with intelligence section police; control of road traffic in the army; administration and control of the Military Police Corps; training of its personnel; command of the military police training school and such other provost and military police duties as may be directed by the Secretary of War.

Appointment of Provost Marshal General and Deputy Provost Marshal General. The provost marshal general and deputy provost marshal general shall be appointed by the President by selection from among the officers of the army.

Appointment and Qualification of Officers. Appointments in the Military Police Corps shall be made by the President by selection from among the officers of the army at large, and from among persons who have held commissions in the armed forces of the United States at any time during the war with Germany; and the provisions of section twenty-seven of the Act of Congress approved February, nineteen hundred and one, are hereby extended to to apply to said officers and to vacancies created in any arm, corps or department of the Army for the detail of officers therefrom to the Military Police Corps. Vacancies thereafter occurring in all grades above that of second lieutenant shall be filled by promotion, according to seniority, from the Military Police Corps.

Appointment by the President. All officers shall be appointed and commissioned by the President, by and with the advice and consent of the Senate, irrespective of the rank or grade held by them on the date of the passage of this Act.

Transfers. Officers of the Military Police Corps and members of the enlisted force may be transferred to other branches of the service without loss of grade by order of the Secretary of War.

Enlisted Men. The enlisted force will be composed of men transferred without loss of grade from the line of the army under such regulations as the Secretary of War shall prescribe.

Promotion of Enlisted Men. Non-commissioned officers of the Military Police Corps will be appointed and promoted in such manner as the Secretary of War shall proscribe. Privates shall have the assimilated rank and wear the insignia of lance corporal and will be respected and obeyed accordingly.

Pay, Allowances, etc. All officers of the Military Police Corps and members of the enlisted force thereof shall receive the same pay and allowances, and be in all respects on the same footing as to pay, allowances and pensions as officers and enlisted men or corresponding grades and length of service in the infantry, except that each enlisted man shall also receive and paid an increase of twenty per centum in the pay of his grade and length of service while serving in the Military Police Corps.

Same.–Payments to be made by disbursing officers, Quartermaster Corps. All officers of the Military Police Corps, and members of the enlisted force thereof shall be paid by Quartermaster Corps disbursing officers from funds appropriated for the pay of the army or transferred to their credit from Military Police Corps appropriations.

Authority of Military Police. Military police in the performance of their duties represent the authority of the commander of the department or organization to which they are attached and will be respected and obeyed accordingly.

Provost Marshal General-Duties. The Provost Marshal General shall have charge, under the direction of the Secretary of War, of all military police duties, and of books, papers and records connected therewith. He is authorized and directed to prepare and enforce, subject to approval of the Secretary of War, rules and regulations for the government of the Military Police Corps, and of all members thereof or persons attached thereto, and to direct and prescribe the kind, number and form of all returns and reports, and to enforce compliance therewith.

Provost Marshal Offices. Such provost marshal and assistant provost marshal offices shall be established, with appropriate furniture and equipment, as shall be directed by the President.

Division of Criminal Investigation. The division of criminal investigation shall be organized from and as part of the Military Police Corps and the enlisted force thereof by the Provost Marshal General for the investigation of crimes committed by members of or against the army.

Training School. A training school for officers and men of the Military Police Corps shall be established and maintained by order of the Secretary of War. A commandant and such commissioned and enlisted personnel as may be necessary will be detailed to duty at the achool by the Provost Marshal General.

Use of Cantonments, Rent of Offices, Purchase of Equipment and Supplies, Administrative Expenses, etc. By order of the President any United States military post, barracks, buildings, camp, cantonment or other establishment, or such part or parts thereof as may be necessary may be used by the military police; buildings or structure constructed; furniture, and other equipment, supplies and appliances purchased; administrative and other needed expenses authorized; and offices rented and equipped, for the use of the Military Police Corps and the enlisted force thereof.

Appropriation for Carrying Into Effect Provisions of Act. For the purpose of carrying this Act into effect the sum of $1, 500,000 is hereby appropriated out of any funds in the Treasury not otherwise appropriated, to be available until June thirtieth, nineteen hundred and twenty.

Appropriation for Expenses of Provost Marshal Offices. Of the sum last above mentioned $100,000, or so much thereof as may be necessary, will be available for the payment of expenses of provost marshal and assistant provost marshal offices, including payment of rent, purchases of furniture and equipment and other expenses connected therewith, under such regulations as the Secretary of War way prescribe.

Appropriation for Military Police Training School. Of the sum hereinbefore appropriated for carrying into effect the provisions of this Act $150,000, or so much thereof as may be necessary, will be available for the payment of rent of buildings, purchase of furniture and equipment and other necessary expenses of the training school for officers and men of the Military Police Corps, under such regulations as the Secretary of War may prescribe.

Appropriation for Criminal Investigation. Of the sum hereinbefore appropriated for carrying into effect the provisions of this Act $200,000, or so much thereof as may be necessary, will be available for the payment of expenses of criminal investigation by the Military Police Corps, including employment of civilian operatives, traveling expenses of operatives, commutation of rations and quarters for officers and men of the division when absent from their stations on duty, and other expenses of criminal investigation, under such regulations as the Secretary of War may prescribe.

Appropriation for Payment of Officers and Enlisted Men of the Military Police Corps. Of the sum hereinbefore appropriated for carrying into effect the provisions of this Act $550,000, or so much thereof as may be necessary, will be available for the pay and allowances of the officers and men of the Military Police Corps not hereby made a part of the line of the army.

Appropriation for Special Equipment for Military Police.

Of the sum hereinbefore appropriated for carrying into effect the provisions of this Act $50,000, or so much thereof as may be necessary, will be available for purchases of special equipment for the Military Police Corps and the enlisted force thereof additional to such equipment as may be available for their use, under such regulations as the Secretary of War may prescribe.

# APPENDIX TWO

## Supreme Council's Instructions to the Inter-Allied Military Mission to Hungary

It will be the object of the Mission:

1st: To get into communication with the Hungarian Government with a view to insuring the observation of the armistice and rendering the disarming effective.

To this end it will be obliged:

(a) To fix the maximum number of effectives of the Hungarian army to be maintained under arms, with the sole object of insuring order in the interior:

(b) To proceed to the disarming of all the demobilized units and to the dissolution of the depôts or mobilizing centers:

(c) To insure the surrender to the Allies of the arms, munitions and war material in excess of the material necessary for the units kept under arms; to include the material coming from the Mackensen Army:

(d) To regulate, in accord with the Allied commands, the distribution of this various material among the Allied Powers interested, taking into account the military effort furnished by each, and the present war situation:

(e) To stop immediately the production of the arsenals and the war manufactures:

2nd: To make a report on the present condition of this matter and its probable outcome:

3rd: To establish liaison with the Commander in Chief of the Roumanian and Serbian armies, in order:

(a) To prevent on the part of the victorious armies all measures which would tend to excite the national sentiment in Hungary or which in any way might prolong the troubled situation in this country and retard the conclusion of peace:

(b) To determine according to the situation of the moment the effectiveness and the emplacements of the Roumanian and Serbian troops that it will be necessary to maintain on Hungarian soil to guarantee order and the execution of the armistice:

(c) To regulate with the Roumanian and Serbian commands the withdrawal of the excess Roumanian and Serbian troops:

The Mission is informed for its further instruction:

1st: That the frontiers of Hungary having been defined already by the Conference and communicated directly to all the Governments concerned, it is the policy of the Conference to withdraw all foreign troops from this country, avoiding all unnecessary delay. It must be noted that the Roumanians have promised to withdraw their armies as soon as the disarming of the Hungarians is accomplished, and in accord with the armistice terms:

2nd: That orders have been given to raise the blockade against Hungary and to proceed to the immediate importation of food stuffs of the most urgent nature:

3rd: That the maintenance of these new conditions will depend on the conduct of the Hungarian Government toward the Allied and Associated Powers:

4th: That these Powers have not the least desire to interfere in the interior affairs of the Hungarian nation concerning the choice of their government, but that at the same time they cannot treat with any government which they cannot trust to carry out fairly its international obligations.

# APPENDIX THREE

## American Military Mission

Members of the American Military Mission in Hungary:

Gen. Harry Hill Bandholtz

Col. Halsey E. Yates, Chairman of the Commission on Police and Gendarmerie

Col. Raymond Sheldon

Col. James Taber Loree

Col. Nathan Horowitz

Lieut. Col. Charles Beatty Moore

Captain Edwin Bulkley Gore

Captain Will Shafroth

Captain Weiss

Lieutenant Laurens M. Hamilton

**Hungarians attached to the American Military Mission**

Lieutenant Count [Paul] Teleki, liaison officer,

M. Emil Zerkowitz, civilian liaison official

M. de Pekár, civilian liaison official, preceding Mr. Zerkowitz

Count Edelsheim, host of General Bandholtz in Budapest.

Twenty-five enlisted soldiers of the Military Police Corps.

# APPENDIX FOUR

## President Wilson's Fourteen Points

I. "Open covenants of peace, openly arrived at, after which there shall be no private international understandings of any kind but diplomacy shall proceed always frankly and in the public view."

II. "Absolute freedom of navigation upon the seas, outside territorial waters, alike in peace and in war, except as the seas may be closed in whole or in part by international action for the enforcement of international covenants."

III. "The removal, so far as possible, of all economic barriers and the establishment of an equality of trade conditions among all the nations consenting to the peace and associating themselves for its maintenance."

IV. "Adequate guarantees given and taken that national armaments will be reduced to the lowest point consistent with domestic safety."

V. "A free, open-minded, and absolutely impartial adjustment of all colonial claims, based upon a strict observance of the principle that in determining all such questions of sovereignty the interests of the populations concerned must have equal weight with the equitable claims of the government whose title is to be determined."

VI. "The evacuation of all Russian territory and such a settlement of all questions affecting Russia as will secure the best and freest cooperation of the other nations of the world in obtaining for her an unhampered and unembarrassed opportunity for the independent determination of her own political development and national policy and assure her of a sincere welcome into the society of free nations under institutions of her own choosing; and, more than welcome, assistance of every kind that she may need and may herself desire. The treatment accorded Russia by her sister nations in the months to come will be the acid test of their good will, of their comprehension of her needs as distinguished from their own interests, and of their intelligent and unselfish sympathy."

VII. "Belgium, the whole world will agree, must be evacuated and restored, without any attempt to limit the sovereignty which she enjoys in common with all other free nations. No other single act will serve as this will serve to restore confidence among the nations in the laws which they have themselves set and determined for the government of their relations with one another. Without this healing act the whole structure and validity of international law is forever impaired."

VIII. "All French territory should be freed and the invaded portions restored, and the wrong done to France by Prussia in 1871 in the matter of Alsace-Lorraine, which has unsettled the peace of the world for nearly fifty years, should be righted, in order that peace may once more be made secure in the interest of all."

IX. "A readjustment of the frontiers of Italy should be effected along clearly recognizable lines of nationality."

X. "The peoples of Austria-Hungary, whose place among the nations we wish to see safeguarded and assured, should be accorded the freest opportunity of autonomous development."

XI. "Rumania, Serbia, and Montenegro should be evacuated; occupied territories restored; Serbia accorded free and secure access to the sea; and the relations of the several Balkan States to one another determined by friendly counsel along historically established lines of allegiance and nationality; and independence and territorial integrity of the several Balkan States should be entered into."

XII. "The Turkish portions of the present Ottoman Empire should be assured a secure sovereignty, but the other nationalities which are now under Turkish rule should be assured an undoubted security of life and an absolutely unmolested opportunity of autonomous development, and the Dardanelles should be permanently opened as a free passage to the ships and commerce of all nations under international guarantees."

XIII. "An independent Polish state should be erected which should include the territories inhabited by indisputably Polish populations, which should be assured a free and secure access to the sea, and whose political and economic independence and territorial integrity should be guaranteed by international covenant."

XIV. "A general association of nations must be formed under specific covenants for the purpose of affording mutual guarantees of political independence and territorial integrity to great and small states alike."

# APPENDIX FIVE

## Letter to General Bandholtz from the American Military Mission, Paris

AMERICAN COMMISSION TO NEGOTIATE PEACE.

Hotel de Crillon, Paris

My dear Bandholtz: September 4, 1919.

I take advantage of the fact that an officer is leaving here tonight for Trieste and thence to Budapest to send you this hasty line.

First of all I want to tell you how very much pleased the entire Commission here is at the splendid work you have been doing in Budapest. By word of mouth from various sources we have full confirmation of what appears in your own reports, namely, that you have been working in full accord with your British colleague even though the representatives of other nations may not have shown the same spirit of cooperation. We have every reason to think that you are the strong man of the Mission. It is to be regretted, - but it cannot be helped, of course, - that your hard and excellent work has not been more fruitful in making our Roumanian friends work inside the traces.

Today (I think) Sir George Clerk, one of Mr. Balfour's personnel, leaves for the purpose of delivering in person to the Roumanian Government a final note of the Allied and Associated Powers. If this is not promptly effective and if the Entente then shows inability or unwillingness to apply further pressure upon the Roumanians, I think it very likely that our Government may relieve you from the Mission of Generals at Budapest, although it may leave you there as an independent observer. We all think that the time has come to make everybody in Europe understand that if they expect further cooperation and assistance from the United States they must play the game properly or we will show them at once that we intend to withdraw completely and leave them to their own resources. I have been trying to get for you an automobile in anticipation of those which have been ordered to be sent to you from the Morgenthau Mission in Poland. Unfortunately, the American Delegation has none that it can send. All of ours have belonged to the American Army and have been sold to the French, and as rapidly as we have no use for one here it has to be turned in to the latter government. But Captain Smythe, who arrived here yesterday with dispatches from Budapest, told me that your own automobile and chauffeur were, as he understands, here and doing nothing. I asked him to go at once and see the proper officer and tell him that it was most desirable that this be at once made available for you. Captain Smythe said that if he could get it he would himself drive the machine to Budapest. In that case I will have time to send you a further and fuller letter.

Meanwhile, I again congratulate you for myself and the American Mission for the excellent work you have been doing in Budapest, I remain

Cordially yours,


(Signed) Tasker H. Bliss

# APPENDIX SIX

## Translation of a Letter from the International Red Cross to the Inter-Allied Commission

We visited Hatvan, Gyongyos, Miskoloz, Sdtoraljg-Ujhely, Nyiregyhaza, Debreczen, Szolnok, Hagyvdrad, Bekde-Gyala, Arad, Temesvdr, Szeged.

In all these towns occupied by the Romanians found an oppression as great as to make life unbearable.

Murder is common, even youths and women are flogged, imprisoned without trial, arrested without any reason. There is theft of personal property under the name of requisition and bribery. In fact a condition of affairs prevails for a Western European to realize who has not seen and heard the evidence.

The people are forced to take the oath of allegiance to the Roumanian King; if they refuse, they are persecuted. Doctors, lawyers, teachers and bank managers are dismissed, they are then deported to their native village if they cannot prove residence of four or five years. They cannot take their furniture with them and often have to leave their families. In some towns they are allowed to remain for payment of a monthly tax to the Roumanians.

Those who remain are not allowed to go to the places where they are likely to get work, so they are forced to take what work they can get. In Arad a county court judge is repairing boots, the teacher of a secondary school, a University man of considerable experiences is now a railway porter. Of the 400 teachers in the county of Arad, only 88 have taken the oath, all others have been dismissed and are now working on farms and doing general laborers work.

Page 2 –

On the Arad – Brad Railway many men, including station master Weber of Brad and the station master of Ketagyhdza have been most fearfully flogged.

On the anniversary of the Roumanian King's birthday they compelled all the Churches to arrange a solemn service and they obliged Hungarian officials to be present. On the same day they ordered all shops to be closed.

Last Good Friday, the Roumanians advanced suddenly to a village called Boros-Sobes and 250 Hungarian soldiers were taken prisoners. These were killed in the most barbarous manner. They were stripped naked and stabbed with bayonets in such a way as to prolong life as long as possible. The Hungarian peasants were then compelled to bury them.

On the Monday following the men of the village were compelled to hand (haul?) railway wagons a distance of 15 kilometres.

At a village near Arad 200 peasants were killed because they resisted having their corn, wheat and agricultural implements taken from them. The village was then simply gutted.

The papers are strictly censored and no free speech is allowed. Not more than three people are allowed to walk together.

The Roumanians have passed a bill in their Parliament in Bucharest which they call a bill of Agrarian Reform. By this bill all land belonging to Hungarians will be bought at a price fixed by the Romanians. This will mean absolute rule, not only to landowners but to the peasants.

The Roumanians have established a Customs-House in every village and town. Delivery permits for goods can only be obtained by the payment of ridiculously large sums. Commerce is impossible.

**Thus ends those two pages.**

# APPENDIX SEVEN

## Newspaper articles published at the close of General Bandholtz's Term in Budapest

The following article appeared in the Pester Lloyd of January 31, 1919, written by Emil Zerkowitz.

"Having fulfilled his Mission, Harry Hill Bandholtz, Brigadier General of the United States Army, the leader of the American Military Mission, will shortly leave Budapest and return to his country and to his home after an absence of nearly two years. The noble-minded and brave General leaves us after having done his work, and we must say that he could not have won a nobler, a more uplifting and happier victory than the one he achieved in Budapest. He conquered the hearts of millions, the love and gratitude and appreciation of the Hungarian nation accompany him on his journey, and we tie a wreath of victory for him out of the flowers of love.

When he arrived in our midst, in the dreary days of the month of August, the country had hardly had time to regain consciousness from a stupor caused by a period of terror when the darkness of renewed horrors covered our souls; the Hungarian capital, occupied by foreign troops, was turned into a death chamber. Armed guards were watching over the downtrodden and tortured national conscience, on the eve of a frightful ordeal. We could not raise cries loud enough, we could not speak openly, for even the winking of our eyes was regarded with suspicion. How could the wide world, the foreign nations and the few friends that we had left and who still retained some humane feeling after a war of five years, a chaotic compound made up from mutual hatred, get to know in what plight we were and what fate was in store for us?

But lo! the world was moved and with it the conscience of triumphant victors. The great powers of the Entente delegated mission of Generals to Budapest; American,

British, Italian and French Military Missions with a general at the head of each of them, who met every day to discuss the position of the occupied country. This was an essentially military function, but it could not maintain its rigidly military character for long. In order to investigate into the damages caused by Roumanian occupation, a Claim Office was set up by the council of the four Generals and placed under the control of the American Mission. In such manner, the American Mission developed into a Mecca, as it were, of the suffering Hungarian pilgrims. It must be admitted that this was a practice that had been adopted by the sufferers long before the Claim Office was brought into being. They hurried to the American Mission hoping for assistance.

Their hopes were not in vain. General Bandholtz, the hardy and brave soldier, was a warm-hearted guardian of the sufferers, the impartial and inexorable judge of injustice, whom nothing could keep from acting, if something was to be done in the interest of a just cause. He persecuted all excesses with unbounded energy and investigated all complaints with inexorable impartiality. He rigorously combated injustice and relieved all innocent sufferers with happy contentment.

He carried into practice all the principles of the much advertised modern diplomacy. He made no secret of what was in his mind, but openly stated his opinion. He was ever ready to discuss matters of importance, but, what is more, he acted. His door was open to all; he received everyone and heard all who wanted to speak to him. This is how he gained a deep insight into the Hungarian soul. He did not limit himself to the study of books or of historical documents, but he turned for information to the data supplied by real life. He made the acquaintance of Count Albert Apponyi, the greatest of our political leaders and often, after discussing with him for hours such questions as were most intimately connected with our very existence, he heard the complaints of some poor farmer, turned out of his property by the troops of occupation. Having been at work all day, he hurried on one occasion late at night to the National Museum to seal its doors with his own hands, thus saving the most valuable treasures of the nation, the precious memorials of its culture and civilization.

He knew us in our suffering and so became the true friend of our nation. It is not mere pity that made him our friend. He proved, by persevering at our side even in our direst catastrophe, a true friend who did not abandon us, but who exhorted our nation to work, our only salvation and the only means to forget. When doing so, he called to our memory our glorious past, and taught us that this nation could not fall a victim to destruction, filled as it is with a keen desire of life, this being the lesson taught by our national history of a thousand years. This is what he said to many of our statesmen and to many journalists who interviewed him, and whoever had an opportunity to get in touch with General Bandholtz could see that his words were prompted by sincere conviction. He will herald these ideas of his, even when he has left the Hungarian capital and when he returns to independent America, his country and the land of George Washington, its Father, of Abraham Lincoln, the liberator of the slaves, and of Thomas Jefferson, the advocate of true democracy. He returns to America, the country where Louis Kossuth, the greatest son of oppressed Hungary, was received in 1851 more warmly and more enthusiastically than any other foreign statesman before or since. America is the country where nearly two million fellow countrymen of ours have found work and a warm reception, the majority of whom have been granted citizens' rights, and where the Magyar is being appreciated, not only for his physical work, but also because of the true virtues of every Hungarian. In America, where there is such a fertile soil for the love of our country and for sympathy, General Bandholtz is sure to become an advocate of our true cause, of our desire to live, and of our faith in the future. His brave collaborators will assist him in his pioneer work. Colonel Loree, who is an incredibly hard worker, an indefatigable, excellent man, who was working for us day and night with love, willingness and self-denial, will be at their head, and so will Colonel Sheldon, this soldier inspired by truly humane ideals, the supporter of all needy people.

The Chief of the Military Mission surrenders his post to the Representative of the American Foreign Department, the Chief of the American Mission, who has just arrived, Mr. U. Grant-Smith. This excellent diplomatist, who worked at Vienna in the service of diplomacy for a number of years, knows our position thoroughly. While taking leave of General Bandholtz with feelings of appreciation and of respect, the public of the country warmly welcomes Mr. Grant- Smith, to whose future work the nation looks with fullest confidence.

And yet our hearts are pained in parting from the General. It is with painful feelings that we see him depart, him, the noble-hearted, excellent gentleman, who, although a soldier, was the first man to make us forget that nations faced each other with arms in hand, nations who used to be united by the traditional feelings of brotherly love, by a community of souls, and by the most glorious human ideals. We want to forget and we are going to forget. But we cannot possibly forget all that we owe to the glorious and noble work of General Bandholtz. On all his ways, our gratitude and undying love will accompany him."

The following is a translation of an article that appeared in the National Journal, Budapest, January 28, 1920:

"This forenoon the American High Commissioner, Mr. Grant-Smith, and General Bandholtz, called on Prime Minister Huszár, who described to them the political and economic situation of the country.

At 1.30 o'clock General Bandholtz and his officers lunched at the Hotel Pannonia as the guests of the Mayor of the City, Mr. Bódy.

"General Bandholtz and the American Military Mission will leave Budapest and the city will always gratefully remember General Bandholtz, because we have so much to thank him for. During the Roumanian occupation, he protected us against the Roumanians' injustice, and it is mainly due to him that they evacuated the country between the Danube and Tisza and also that they did not rob our museums. The General himself sealed the National Museum and it was the American Mission that prevented the Roumanians from delivering the Bolshevists.

"It is General Bandholtz also who revived interest in charity work in Hungary."

The following is a translation of an article which appeared in the Hungarian newspaper Uj Nemzedék, January 29, 1920.

"The members of the American Military Mission and their chief, General Bandholtz, are soon leaving our capital, probably about the fifteenth of February. The affairs of the Mission are now being handed over to the American High Commissioner. The Magyars will always remember General Bandholtz with the feelings of deepest gratitude, as there is such a lot we must be thankful for to him and to the Mission. In the days of our profound sorrow, during the occupation of our country by the Roumanians, it was he who stood up for our righteous cause, and we don't know of any instance when he did not defend us. General Bandholtz persuaded the Roumanians to evacuate Transdanubia and the territories between the Danube and the Tisza, and it is owing to him that the Roumanians did not pillage our museums. The General personally sealed the entrance of our National Museum. Also we owe it to the energetic intervention of the Mission, that the Roumanians' endless efforts to liberate arrested Communists were frustrated. It was General Bandholtz who initiated the American actions of benevolence and hereby dried a sea of tears on the Hungarian faces."

# SELECTED BIBLIOGRAPHY

"A Brief History of West Point," West Point Online. http://www.usma.edu/history.asp

"A Concise History of Hungary," Miklos Molnar, Cambridge University Press

"Aguinaldo: A Narrative of Filipino Ambitions," E. Wildman 1901, Norwood Press, Norwood, MA

"A Leap to Arms - The Cuban Campaign of 1898," by Jack Cameron Dierks, J. B. Lippincott and Co.

"A Life of Duty-The Autobiography of George Wilcox McIver 1858-1947, James Dembo. Editor, The History Press 2006

"American Hungarian Relations 1918-1944," by Mark Imre Major, Danubian Press 1974

"A Model for Studying World War II Era LCMS in the Archaeological Record," by Matthew E. Keith, Master Thesis, U. of South Florida, Tampa, FL

"An Ancient Amphibious Assault," by Commander Edgar K. Thompson, USN, US Naval Institute Proceedings, Jan 1947

"Apache prisoners of war at Alabama's Mount Vernon Barracks," by Jerry A. Davis, 1887-1894, Alabama Review, Oct 1999.

"Army Surveillance in America, 1775-1980, by Joan M, Jensen, Yale University Press 1991

"A Splendid Little War," Online History of the Spanish-American War, http://www.homeofheroes.com/wallofhonor/spanish_am/01_intro.html

"Army Surveillance in America, 1775-1980," by Joan M. Jensen, Yale University Press, 1991

Bandholtz Obit, USMA Association of Graduates, Superintendant's Report 1927

Bandholtz Papers, Bentley Research Library, University of Michigan

Bandholtz Papers, Hungarian National Museum, Budapest, Hungary

"Battle of El Caney," New York Times, July 18, 1898

"Biography of Major General Harry Hill Bandholtz 1864-1925," by Grafton H. Cook II, July 2005, unpublished

"Buffalo Soldier Regiment: History of the Twenty-fifth United StatesInfantry, 1869-1926 (Blacks in the American West)," by John Nankivell, U of Nebraska Press, 2001

Catalogue, Officers and Students, Michigan Agricultural College, for the year 1896-7, published by the college (now Michigan State Univ)

:Combates y Capiulacion de Santiago", by Tejeira Jose Muller, Madrid, 1898

"Cruelty of Filipinos, The NY Times, September 27, 1907

"Evolution of the Office of the Provost Marshal General", by Ronald Craig, Military Police-The Professional Bulletin, April 2004

"Friends of Fort Niagara Website, Http://www.fortontario.com/History/History.html

"Great Excitement at Augusta; Minnesota Soldiers Riotous," Atlanta Constitution, Feb 6, 1899

"Greater Roumania," by Charles Upson Clark, Dodds Mead and Co., NY, 1922

"Harry Hill Bandholtz 1864-1925, United States Army," by Grafton H. Cook II, unpublished.

"History of the 29th Division," by John A. Cutchins, Press of MacCalla & Co, Philadelphia 1921

"How I carried the Letter to Garcia,, by Col. Andrew S. Rowan, US Naval Academy Website. http://homeport.usnaweb.org/howicarried.html

"Jungle Patrol – The Story of the Philippine Constabulary," by Vic Hurley, E. P. Dutton & Co., Inc. 1938

"St Joseph's County – Historic River Country," by Jane Simon Ammeson, Arcadia Publishing

NY Evening Telegram, 6 March 1919, "Men Made by the War," by Jane Dixon – Bandholtz Papers, UMICH)

"Keeping the Spirit of 1896 Alive," by Onofre D. Corpuz, Ph.D., U of Philippines http://www.bibingka.com/phg/misc/spirit96.htm

"King Ferdinand Now in Budapest," The NY Times, August 9, 1919

"Lustgarten Convicted of $20,000 Swindle," Brooklyn Daily Standard Union, July 31, 1919

"Macario Sakay: Tulisan or Patriot?," by Paul Flores, Philippine Centennial Series. http://www.bibingka.com/phg/sakay/default.htm

"Magyar Mission in Paris," NY Times, Feb 12, 1920

"Manual for the Provost Marshal General's Department, AEF, 1919," Bandholtz Papers, University of Michigan

"Medal of Honor Recipients, Spanish American War," US Army Center of Military History, http://www.history.army.mil/html/moh/warspain.html

"Meddling in Middle Europe: Britain and the Lands Between, 1919-1925, by Miklos Lojko, Central Europe Press, 2005

Memo dated Dec 3, 1919, and an untitled document dated Budapest Dec 6, 1919, from the Hungarian Military Archives, Budapest

"Mingo Miners Fight With Police-Five Miners Fall," NY Times, Aug 29, 1921

"Military Police," by Robert K. Wright, Jr., Army Lineage Series, US Army Military History Institute 1992

"Minnesota in the Spanish-American War and Philippine Insurrection," published by Minnesota War Commission, dated 1923

"Minnesota Soldiers Riotous," Atlanta Constitution, Feb 9, 1899

"90,000 Pay Honor to Our Unknown Lying in State," NY Times, November 11, 1921

"Origins of the Military Police, by Jacob B. Lishchiner, Military Affairs, Vol XI No. 2, 1947, US Army Military History Institute

"Paris 1919," by Margaret MacMillan, Random House 2001

Personal letters of Corporal Norris Ball, 23rd Engineers, AEF, to his family in Colorado, dated 1918-1919, from the collection of Allan E. Barnett

"Philippines: A Country Study. Washington: Ronald E. Dolan, ed, GPO for the Library of Congress, 1991.

"Regular and Volunteer Dishonorably Discharged," The Augusta Chronicle, Feb 9, 1899

"Report of the Provost Marshal General A.E.F. for 1919," US Military Academy Library, West Point, NY

"Regulations for Provost Marshal General's Department, AEF in France," Dec 9, 1917, US Army Military History Institute

"Report on Examination of the Coal Deposits on Polillo Island," Annual Reports of the War Department, Volume XIII, Part 4, US Government Printing Office 1905

"Report of the Provincial Governor of Tayabas," by H. H. Bandholtz, Jan 15, 1903

"Reports of the Philippine Commission to the Secretary of War," Government Printing Office

"Report of the Philippine Exposition Board," to the Louisiana Purchase Exposition, St Louis, 1904

"Rumanians in Hungary,", The NY Times, February 21, 1920

"Soldier Killed in Augusta," Atlanta Constitution Newspaper, Feb 5, 1899

"Soldiers and Patriots, Buffalo Soldiers and Afro-Cubans in Tampa, 1898," by Brent R. Weisman, July 1999, U. of South Florida Anthropology Department

"Spanish American War," by Daniel E. Brannen, Jr., Thompson-Gale, 2003

"Tampa, Florida and the Spanish-American War of 1898: A Chronology," by Paul Eugen Camp, U. of South Florida

"Text of Amendment to Draft Regulations Announced by Provost Marshal General," The Washington Post, May 24, 1918

"The Admirable Admiral – Ricard. Byrd," by Warren H. Deck, Masonic Americana 1976, pgs 201-203

"The Annotated Memoirs of Admiral Milklos Horthy, Regent of Hungary, by Miklos Horthy, 1957

"The Battle of Blair Mountain," by Robert Shogan, Westview Press, Boulder, CO 2004

"The Cable Cutters of Cienfuegos," by Carlos C. Hanks, US Naval Institute Proceedings, Mar 1931

"The Country that I Love, by Marie, Queen of Roumania," Duckworth, London, 1925

"The Development of Naval Gunfire Support of Amphibious Operations," by Captain L. E. McMillan, USN, US Naval Institute Proceedings, Jan 1948

"The Hostage," by W. E. B. Griffin, G. P. Putnam & Sons, NY, 2005

"The Korean Expedition of 1871," by K. Jack Bauer, US Naval Institute Proceedings, Feb 1948

"The Last Romantic-The Life of the Legendary Marie, Queen of Roumania," Hannah Pakula, Simon and Shuster

"The Last Salute: Civil and Military Funeral, 1921-1969, by B. C. Mossman and M. W. Stark, US Government Printing Office, 1991

"The Martial Spirit," by Walter Millis, The Riverside Press, 1931

"The 1920-21 Deflation: The Role of Aggregate Supply, by J. R. Vernon; Economic Inquiry, Vol. 29, 1991

"The Odyssey of the 15th Minnesota," the Spanish American War Centennial Website

"The Philippines: Past and Present," (Vol. 1) by Dean C. Worcester

"The Philippines: Story of Insurrection," by Dr. Stephen Jess, SW Michigan College

"The Role of Florida in the Spanish-American War, 1898," by William J. Schellings, doctoral dissertation, University of Florida

"The Story of the Philippines," by Murat Halstead, Our Possessions Publishing Co., Chicago

"The United States Army and the Return to Normalcy in Labor Dispute Interventions: The Case of the West Virginia Coal Mine Wars, 1920-1921, by Clayton D. Laurie,

"The World's Machine Guns in the Great War, by P. V. Garland, Emma Gee Summer 2002," Machine Gun Corps Old Comrades Association, London

"The United States Army and the Return to Normalcy in Labor Dispute Interventions: The Case of the West Virginia

Coal Mine Wars, 1920-1921," by Clayton D. Laurie, West Virginia History Magazine, Volume 50, 1991

"True Tales of the D.C.I.", by Karl W. Detzer, The Bobbs-Merrill Company, 1923

US Army, G.O. 127, Hqs., Dept of Army, Court of Inquiry, dated July 8, 1890

"United Roumania," by Charles Upson Clark, Dodds, Mead and Co., NY, 1932

US Military Academy Archives, West Point, NY

# AUTHOR BIOGRAPHY

Patrick V. Garland was born in New York City, in January 1937. He was the fifth child to Mary McConville, of Scotland, and Christopher Garland, of Ireland. The family grew to eight children and an assortment of pets.

Raised in Kings County (Brooklyn), Pat attended Catholic elementary and public high schools. At age 17, he enlisted in the United States Army, to follow an older brother. Pat initially trained as an airborne infantry soldier, and later trained as a Military Policeman, during 1957. This transition introduced him to a career field he learned to love. Advancing through the ranks, he trained for a position as Special Agent of the Army's Criminal Investigation Division, graduating as "distinguished graduate." He served in Criminal Investigation Division duties until 1967.

It was then that Pat applied for, and was accepted for highly specialized training as a Forensic Scientist, specializing in Firearms Identification. Forensic Ballistics, as it is more commonly known, was to become his life's major career. In 1973, being the first Army forensic scientist to be elected President of the Association of Firearms and Toolmark Examiners, an international society of his peers, honored Pat.

Retiring from the US Army's Criminal Investigation Laboratory System in 1974, Pat remained in the forensic science field, working for the Virginia Bureau of Forensic Science, Tennessee Bureau of Investigation, and the Crime Laboratory of the Broward County Sheriff's Department, in Florida. Another distinct honor came in 1976, with being selected for a panel of seven, to re-examine the firearms evidence related to the Assassination of Senator Robert F. Kennedy. Pat retired totally from his chosen field after a nine-month 1995 Department of Justice contract, to examine evidence in multiple shootings in the Washington, D.C. area.

Living in a Florida community, with his wife of 41 years, Pat devotes his time to traveling the world, researching history, and writing for military publications. This is his first book project.